CONTENTS

GARDEN BIRDS DIRECTORY
This section of the book (pages 26-55) provides detailed character descriptions of the 30 most common garden birds that you are likely see, giving details of their appearance, dietary preferences, nesting habits and other distinctive features.

HOUSE SPARROW

DUNNOCK

STARLING

BLACKBIRD

SONG THRUSH

ROBIN

RARER VISITORS
The final 12 entries (pages 56-61) feature rarer garden visitors which you may also be fortunate enough to see.

CHAFFINCH

JLLFINCH 33

WREN 40

GREEN WOODPECKER 47

PIED WAGTAIL 54

REDSTART 58

ENFINCH 34

TREECREEPER 41

ROOK 48

SPOTTED FLYCATCHER 55

FIELDFARE 59

LDFINCH 35

NUTHATCH 42

JACKDAW 49

TAWNY OWL 56

REDWING 59

BLUE TIT 36

COLLARD DOVE 43

MAGPIE 50

LITTLE OWL 56

BLACKCAP 60

REAT TIT 37

WOOD PIGEON 44

JAY 51

BARN OWL 57

MARSH TIT 60

COAL TIT 38

TOWN PIGEON 45

HOUSE MARTIN 52

WAXWING 57

SPARROWHAWK 61

-TAILED 39 TIT

GR. SPOTTED 46 WOODPECKER

SWALLOW 53

SISKIN 58

KESTREL 61

ENJOYING GARDEN BIRDS

The world would not end if all the birds were to disappear, but it would be a very different and much duller place. Our gardens would certainly be a lot less interesting and also less productive without the presence of birds, because they consume immense numbers of caterpillars and other insects that would otherwise damage or even destroy our plants and crops. Blue tits scouring bark crevices in the winter, for example, are destroying the eggs of blackfly and other aphids and reducing the likelihood of destructive outbreaks in the spring. Even city-dwellers would soon notice the lack of birds, although they may at the same time appreciate the greater cleanliness of buildings resulting from the lack of pigeon and starling droppings.

BIRDS ARE FUN

In addition to appreciating their economic contribution, our garden birds give us great pleasure with their songs and also with their amusing antics as they squabble over scraps of food or play tug-of-war with bits of nesting material. The idea of waking up to a land where no birds sing is distinctly unappealing. Furthermore there is evidence that watching and listening to birds can actually improve our well-being. The contemplation of nature definitely has a comforting and relaxing effect, and many doctors agree that hospital patients able to see the countryside and watch birds from their windows recover more quickly than those who look at nothing but brick walls.

THE BIRDS BENEFIT

Bird-gardening is a reciprocal process – the birds need us just as much as we need them. Birds, in common with many other forms of wildlife, are getting a raw deal these days as their natural homes and feeding grounds are destroyed to make way for new roads and houses. But here gardens can help: they are one of the few habitats that are on the increase and, covering an estimated million hectares of Britain, they serve as important nature reserves, especially if you fill them with the right kinds of shrubs and other plants.

Nevertheless, some of our birds, including some that were once common garden species, have become noticeably rarer in recent years. For birds, gardens are not natural habitats and, however well they are stocked with plants, they cannot provide all that the birds need. They need as much help as you can give them. Providing a range of foods to augment those that are found naturally in the garden is a major part of bird-gardening and can turn your garden into a vital refuelling station for the birds. If you provide a variety of suitable nesting sites as well, you may find that some of the birds take up residence and make your garden their home.

You will only see a small proportion of Britain's 550 or so

Right: What could be better for a great tit – a comfortable home in a well-stocked garden!

native bird species in your garden, but over the year you could well receive visits from 20 or 30 species. Enjoy your gardening and enjoy your birds.

Far left: *The robin is one the tamest of our garden birds.*
Left: *Bird cherry produces a crop of bird-friendly fruits.*

A BIRD-FRIENDLY GARDEN

Every garden gets a few bird visitors, even if these are confined to the occasional pigeon or house sparrow, but by growing the right kinds of plants and putting out an assortment of foods you can persuade a surprising variety of birds to become regular visitors. Some of them may settle down and breed so giving you an even greater reward for your efforts.

SHRUBS FOR FOOD AND SHELTER

A few shrubs or small trees, especially if planted in a clump, can give a really natural atmosphere to a garden and make the birds feel at home. But choose carefully: trees grow tall, and what might fit neatly into your garden at first might turn into a giant problem. Native species are best because they support lots of insects, and most birds, including those that are essentially seed-eaters, need insects to feed their nestlings. Hawthorn, rowan, bird cherry, crab apple, holly and guelder rose all attract birds with their colourful autumn fruits, and most have cheerful flowers earlier in the year. Red currant fruits are especially attractive to blackbirds in the summer. Birch is an excel-

Above: The starling, one of our commonest garden birds, will eat almost anything. This youngster will soon gets its speckled adult coat.

lent tree for the garden – elegant and not casting a lot of shade, but yielding lots of seed for the finches. Hazel is a great favourite with the nuthatch and the woodpeckers, and you can eat the nuts yourself. But don't ignore the exotic shrubs altogether: the evergreen *Photinia davidii* provides shelter through out the year as well as berries in the autumn, and bees adore its nectar in the spring. Look in the surrounding countryside or neighbouring gardens to see what sorts of shrubs might do well in your area.

HOMES IN THE HEDGE

If you are lucky enough to have a garden hedge, you may well find blackbirds, dunnocks, and song thrushes nesting in it. Let brambles and honeysuckle scramble over it to provide extra food. And go easy with the hedge-trimmer, especially i the nesting season. The most bird-friendly gardens are alway a little untidy, so don't be afraid to let grasses grow up at the bottom of the hedge: their seeds will keep

Below and below centre: A blackbird enjoys a paddle in the bird bath, while a song thrush contemplates a dip in the garden pond.

Above: Goldfinches like seeding dandelions, and they often rip them out before they are ripe.

many birds happy and their leaves will feed numerous caterpillars – more bird food.

If you don't have a hedge, why not plant one? It need not be at the edge of the garden: a low hedge makes a good screen for the vegetable plot. Put in as many species as you can and perhaps give it a wavy outline for a more natural look.

FLOWERS FOR BIRDS

Few birds actually eat flowers, but tasty insects abound in the flower beds, and the seeds that follow the flowering season are eagerly sought out by many birds. Sunflowers, teasels, cornflowers, and some of the cultivated thistles all yield plenty of seed and you can have fun watching the birds tugging them out. If you have a spare

corner, let the dandelions take over: the flowers make a bright splash in the spring and goldfinches love the seeds.

VARIETY IS THE SPICE OF LIFE

The greater the variety of plants and habitats that you can accommodate in your garden, the greater the variety of birds and other wildlife that are likely to drop in. A pile of old logs, full

of slugs and creepy-crawlies, is a great hunting place. A pond is also a wonderful attraction, giving birds the chance to bathe and drink. It might draw in the biggest garden visitor – the heron although you won't want to see this if you have fish in your pond. Avoid the temptation to cover large areas with decking or paving stones: there is evidence that the craze for these low-maintenance gardens has contributed to the decline of house sparrows and other birds in many urban and suburban areas by denying them the insects that they need for their youngsters.

However varied your garden is, the birds will still appreciate additional food, especially in the winter time. And don't forget the water. If you don't have a pond, you can provide water in small containers. Birds can't drink ice, so replace the water regularly in cold weather.

THE BIRDS' DAY

Most of our garden birds are early risers, usually up and about long before we are unless the weather is really nasty. Their lives are governed largely by the Sun, most of them waking at dawn and going to sleep at dusk.

THE DAWN CHORUS

At the start of the breeding season male birds spend a lot of time singing to attract mates. You can hear them singing at any time of the day at this time of the year, but as soon as the birds have paired up and built their nests their singing is restricted to certain times of the day, most famously the hour or so around dawn. As soon as they wake, the males start to sing to warn other birds that the territories are occupied and that they should keep away. Some native birds can be heard as early as March, but for the full dawn chorus you must wait until the summer visitors add their voices in May. You can hear it before 4 o'clock on a fine morning, although it usually starts later on overcast days.

Below: A blue tit must catch many insects during the course of a day. This one has taken a crane-fly.

Above: The robin's cheerful song can be heard well into the evening, even in wintertime.

Not all the birds start at the same time. The song thrush is one of the first of our garden birds to burst into song, followed by the blackbird and the wren. The seed-eating species tend to join in somewhat later, and the robin is also a late starter – perhaps because it also goes to bed late.

The dawn chorus lasts for no more than an hour or so at full volume and gradually dies away during the morning as the birds get down to the serious business of feeding themselves and their families. Things are usually fairly quiet in the middle of the day, but then the chorus starts up again towards evening, although evensong is never as loud or rich as the dawn chorus.

FOOD, FOOD, FOOD

During the nesting season the birds have to work very hard to feed themselves and their offspring. Great tits feeding well-grown nestlings have been seen bringing caterpillars and other food to the nest more or less every minute, and they keep it up throughout the hours of daylight – perhaps as much as 17 hours every day. Life is not quite so frantic outside the breeding season, but the birds still need to feed themselves. In summer and autumn, when the weather is fairly warm, the tits may spend about 75 per cent of the daylight hours feeding, mainly in the morning and the evening. The birds need more food in the winter

in order to keep themselves warm, but there is less time in which to find it and they may spend over 90 per cent of the daylight hours searching for food.

AND SO TO BED

As the sky darkens towards nightfall, most of our garden birds start to look for somewhere to roost or sleep. Nests are not normally slept in outside the breeding season, although wrens and house sparrows don't know this – they often use their nests throughout the year and even make additional nests in which to roost. Other birds find sheltered spots, usually in dense vegetation, and settle down for the night. They pull in their extremities and, with their feathers fluffed up around them like duvets, they manage to keep reasonably warm during the hours of darkness.

Below: The beautiful barn owl can be seen and heard over many rural and suburban gardens.

Above: The song thrush usually starts off the dawn chorus with its fine, melodious song.

COMMUNAL ROOSTS

Although many birds roost alone, the nightly roost can be a real social occasion for some species. Starlings are famous, or perhaps infamous, for their huge roosts, for which they start to prepare in the middle of the afternoon. Family groups that might have been feeding in neighbouring gardens join forces and fly off towards the regular roost. Birds from other villages gradually link up until thousands of birds are on the wing, all with the same goal. This might be a wood or a park or some city buildings, and when they reach it the birds make an awful lot of noise before settling down for the night. They are also messy and so these roosting flocks are unwelcome in built-up areas.

FLY-BY-NIGHTS

The owls are among the very few birds that are active at night. They wake at dusk and take over from the hawks and kestrels. Incredibly sensitive eyes and ears enable them to detect mice and voles on the darkest nights, and soft feathers allow them to swoop down and snatch their victims with hardly a sound. By the time the day-flying birds are waking up, the owls are on their perches and fast asleep.

AN INTERNAL CLOCK

Although their lives are regulated largely by the Sun, birds do have a built-in sense of time. If you put food out at a certain time every day the birds will soon cotton on to this and will know exactly when to come. If you are slightly late one day, you will probably find them waiting for you.

WHAT'S ON THE MENU?

Our garden birds are grateful for almost any food that you care to throw out for them, but kitchen scraps and left-overs do not give them all that they need. Bread, for example, can provide much-needed energy during the winter, but its nutritional value is limited – so don't let the birds have too much. If you really want to attract and enjoy your garden birds, it is worth spending a bit of time and money to give them both quality and variety. Remember that not all birds have the same tastes, so give them as much variety as you can. Uncooked porridge oats, suet, mashed potato, dried fruit, grated cheese (not too strong), cake, and pastry (cooked or uncooked) are all valuable foods. Many birds will also enjoy over-ripe or damaged fruit, which can sometimes be obtained very cheaply or even free from shops and market stalls.

Above: Birds love to rip out the ripening seeds of sunflowers.

SEED MIXTURES

Wild bird food, containing assorted seeds, can be bought from most pet shops and from many other stores. Most of it is excellent, but beware the cheaper mixtures. These contain a high proportion of wheat and barley grains which, although good for pigeons and pheasants, are of little value to our smaller birds. Specialist firms supply a wide range of seed mixtures, each designed for particular groups of birds and providing the right balance of energy-rich and growth-promoting nutrients. 'Soft-bill' mixtures contain crushed grain and seeds of various kinds, often mixed with sultanas and dried mealworms, and these are perfect for robins and thrushes and other birds whose beaks are not designed to deal with hard seeds.

You can even buy seed mixtures formulated to cater for differing energy requirements at different times of the year. The energy content of the food is very important, especially in the winter when more energy is needed to keep warm. Birds may consume up to half their own weight of food each day.

PEANUTS FOR ENERGY

Peanuts are full of oil and are an excellent source of energy, but should never be offered in such a way that the birds can make off with whole nuts. They

Left: A peanut feeder will attract many kinds of birds, especially the tits and finches.

should be presented in one or more of the many feeders that enable the birds to get no more than small pieces at a time – and then there will be no risk of their trying to ram whole nuts down their nestlings' throats. Be sure to get good quality peanuts from reliable sources. Cheap nuts of inferior quality may contain a dangerous poison, called aflatoxin, derived from moulds infecting the nuts.

SUNFLOWER POWER

Sunflower seeds also provide loads of energy. Black ones are best because their coats are thin and easily broken open. You can also buy de-husked sunflower seeds, commonly known as sunflower hearts.

These are a bit more expensive than the complete seeds, but every scrap is edible: the birds don't have to expend energy opening them and you don't have to sweep up the husks.

NUTRITIOUS MEALWORMS

Mealworms – the grubs of a dark brown beetle – are an excellent source of protein and eagerly taken by many birds, including the robin. You can buy them from pet shops and bird food suppliers and put them in a dish on the bird-table a few at a time. Once you have a supply, you can keep a colony of mealworms going for years. Keep them in a biscuit tin or an earthenware jar

with a cloth cover and keep them well supplied with cream crackers or crispbread – but do keep them dry. Moisture will allow mould to develop and kill the insects. Sieve the contents from time to time to eliminate the powdery droppings. Feed the excess adults to your birds as well. You can also buy freeze-dried mealworms, which are excellent ingredients for bird pudding.

HOW TO MAKE A BIRD PUDDING

A fun way to present food, for birds and bird-watchers alike, is in what is commonly known as a bird pudding. You can use ingredients such as cheese, dried fruit, dried mealworms, biscuit crumbs, cereals, seeds, and all manner of kitchen scraps and left-overs apart from vegetables.

2

3

Mix the ingredients well in a bowl (**1**). Melt a quantity of dripping or lard and pour it over the other ingredients in the bowl (**2**). Mix it well and allow it to set.

Then you can fill individual smaller containers with it (**3**), or just turn it out on the bird-table and watch the birds demolish it. You can push pieces of the

pudding into a nut log (see page 17), or you can also mould the pudding into balls and hang them up by passing a piece of string through each one.

DISHING UP THE FOOD

Look in any pet shop or wildlife catalogue and you will find an amazing array of feeding devices, designed to serve a wide variety of foods to an equally wide variety of birds. The prices also vary a great deal and what you buy is very much a matter of personal taste. Many feeders are undoubtedly designed to appeal to the bird-watcher rather than the birds: the birds don't mind what the feeders look like as long as they deliver the goods!

Above: A nuthatch is about to try a tasty fat ball. These balls, whether bought or made at home, attract many birds.

FEED REGULARLY

Whatever kind of feeder you choose for your garden, it is essential to keep it well stocked. Once you start feeding your birds, they will quickly cotton on and come regularly to the feeding station – and if there is nothing there, they will hang about in hope, wasting time and energy that could have been used to find food elsewhere. In cold weather many of them could die. If you plan a long holiday, either get some large-capacity feeders or ask a neighbour to top up your regular feeders.

KEEP IT CLEAN

Bird-feeders get dirty in use: scraps of food that cannot be reached gradually rot, and the birds' droppings inevitably soil trays and perches. A build-up of dirt can damage the birds' health, so clean your feeders regularly with an anti-bacterial surface cleaner such as you might use in your own kitchen or dining room.

Above: Many birds love coconuts. Saw a nut in half and hang each half from a branch or from your bird-table. Blue tits and other birds will give you hours of fun as they chip away at the flesh. But **never** give your birds desiccated coconut.

Right: Outwitting squirrels is not easy, for they can climb and leap and even walk tightropes. There are, however, a number of squirrel-proof feeders on the market. Many of them employ an outer cage with a mesh that allows birds to get in but keeps the squirrels out. This one has a cylindrical 'shutter' that slides down over the food as soon as a squirrel sets foot on the feeder.

Below left: A squirrel baffle fixed over a nut basket prevents squirrels from attacking the nuts from above and also keeps the food dry.

Above right: If your nut basket is mounted on a pole, the baffle can be fitted below it, to outwit any marauding cats as well as squirrels.

Above: Hung from a tree or a wall bracket, or suspended from your bird-table, this simple cage is the ideal peanut-dispenser. The stainless steel mesh prevents the birds from removing whole nuts, so they have to stay for dinner as they peck the nuts into smaller fragments. Peanuts are commonly sold in plastic nets, but it is not a good idea to hang these up because the birds can get their feet caught in the mesh: empty the nuts into a feeder.

Above right: Tubular feeders made of tough plastic are designed to serve up smaller seeds. They come in various sizes, with varying numbers of feeding ports, allowing several birds to feed together. They also keep the food dry. This chaffinch is enjoying a feed at one of the ports. Special feeders are available for dispensing niger seeds. Also referred to as nyjer and thistle seeds, these seeds are very small, but they are packed with energy and well worth offering to your birds.

Goldfinches love them (see page 35). Most of these tubular feeders can be mounted on poles as well as hung from branches, and they are also available with suction pads that allow you to fix them onto your window panes.

BUILD A FEEDING STATION

You don't have to be a master carpenter to make a traditional bird-table. All you really need to provide is a flat surface on top of a pole. The table top can be cut from a piece of blockboard and it should be at least 50cm square, so that several birds can feed at the same time without too much squabbling – although a bit of argument can be fun to watch. It should have a rim around the edge to stop the food from blowing away in the wind, but be sure to leave a small gap in each corner so that rain can run away: birds like and need water but you are not making a paddling pool for them! Some people like to put a roof on their bird-tables. This might look pretty, but the birds don't have such protection when feeding in the wild and a roof can actually deter some birds. It can also interrupt your view and make photography more difficult.

Above: Some tits are enjoying a nourishing feed of bird pudding served up in a nut log.

The post should be at least 150cm high to make it hard for cats to reach the top – but not so high that you can't clean the table or put food on it easily. Although rustic posts look nice, cats and squirrels can climb them easily. A smooth metal pole made from a length of scaffolding is safer. Alternatively, if you are troubled by cats and squirrels, you can fit a baffle below the table.

By adding arms to the post or the platform, you can make your table into a complex feeding station, from which you can hang a variety of commercial or home-made feeding devices. But do not add so many feeders that the birds get in each other's way.

If you don't have a suitable spot for a free-standing table, you can fix one to a wall or a tree trunk with a couple of brackets. You can even fix a tray to a window-sill, and then you will almost have the birds indoors with you.

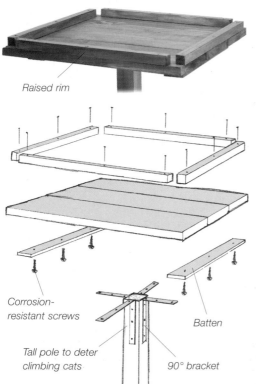

Raised rim

Corrosion-resistant screws

Batten

Tall pole to deter climbing cats

90° bracket

Left: Your table can be made from two or three planks that are secured together, as shown here, or from a single piece of board.

GROUND FEEDING

Many birds, including dunnocks and song thrushes, prefer to feed on the ground and ignore even the best-stocked bird table. You can cater for them with a ground-feeding station. This is simply a bird table without a pole! You can of course scatter food directly on the ground, but small seeds will then be lost, especially in rainy weather. Ground feeding is obviously out if your garden suffers from cats.

LUNCH IN A LOG

A nut log is a good bird-table accessory that might attract woodpeckers and nuthatches. All you need is a cylindrical log or even a length of sawn timber about 30cm long. Drill some holes in it about a centimetre deep and about the same in diameter. These will take peanuts or raisins, or you can simply fill them with fat or bird pudding. Peanut butter can also be served in the logs. A screw eye in one end will allow you to hang the log in a tree as well as from the bird-table.

DAILY BREAD

House sparrows and some other birds enjoy tucking into a slice of bread from time to time, and by presenting the bread in a simple home-made feeder you can watch them feed instead of just watching

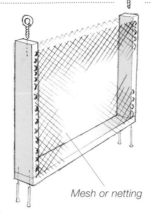

Mesh or netting

Above: *If you use plastic mesh for your bread feeder, use a rigid type so that the birds do not catch their feet in it.*

them fly away with it. You need a short length of batten 1-2cm thick and some fine-mesh wire or plastic netting. Cut and shape the batten into a U-shaped frame and staple the netting to both sides, making sure that there are no sharp edges. Stick a slice of bread into the finished feeder, hang it up, and watch the fun. For an extra treat, stick a slice of bird pudding into the feeder – but only on cold days: the pudding melts in warm weather.

A FEEDER FOR FRUIT

Apples scattered on the ground attract lots of birds, but you can make the birds work a bit harder for their daily fruit with this ingenious feeder made from four lengths of wood arranged in a square as illustrated. Carefully drill through the vertical sides of the square to make a hole large enough to take a knitting needle or a kebab skewer. Drill another

hole through the bottom edge to take a piece of dowel that will provide a perch on each side for the birds to stand on. A piece of cord and a couple of screw eyes at the top will enable you to hang the device from a convenient branch. And then all you need to do is to fix the apple in place by passing the needle or skewer through it and sit back and watch as the birds come to enjoy the fruit.

Dowel perch

Above: *You can also serve fat balls in here, but only in cold weather when the fat will not melt.*

THE NESTING SEASON

Unless your garden contains mature trees, thick hedges, or dense shrubs it is not likely to provide many natural nesting sites for birds. You can, nevertheless, encourage some birds to settle down and breed by erecting nest-boxes. You will find an amazing range of these in mail-order catalogues, pet shops, and garden centres, although there are really only two basic designs – the tit-box and the open-fronted box. The tit-box has a relatively small entrance hole and is aimed at the tits and other species that habitually nest in tree holes. The open-fronted box is exactly that – a box with the front partly or completely removed – and it is used by a wide range of birds, including robins and flycatchers. Both types of box come in a range of sizes and, between them, they will satisfy pretty well all of the species likely to nest in your garden. Nest-boxes are traditionally made of wood, but increasing numbers are now being made from cement and sawdust mixtures. These are particularly good because they provide excellent insulation without condensation and they are virtually rot-proof. Avoid plastic nest-boxes because these suffer from condensation problems inside.

SITING IS ALL-IMPORTANT

Nest-boxes can be fixed to walls, trees, fences, or pergolas and must always be firmly attached. You will obviously want to watch the birds' comings and goings from your window, but never site nest-boxes where they will be exposed to the mid-day sun, which can quickly turn a comfortable nest-box into an oven. Open-fronted boxes are most likely to be use if they are concealed among creepers. You won't see much activity at the nest but a landing stage in the form of a simple post a

metre or so away might help: the birds may well land there first and then you will be able

Above: Great tits have nested i this traditional tit box. The youngster being fed is very nearly ready to fly. Box designs vary a great deal. This one has removable side for cleaning.
Left: Spotted flycatchers are nesting in this open-fronted box which is fitted into a safe corne. The box is also a good vantage point from which to spot passing insects.

to see what food is being taken to the nest. Beware of cats, and site your boxes out of their reach – at least two metres high and not on climbable trees.

Get your nest-boxes up early so that the birds have plenty of time to get used to them and examine them before the nesting season. They are best put up in the winter, and certainly no later than mid-February. In the autumn, when the breeding season is well and truly over, you can open your

and dry grass. Peanut feeders make good containers, from which the birds can easily extract what they want. A basket of fine twigs will also be appreciated. If the birds can find their nesting materials close at hand they will have more energy for nest-building and egg-laying.

support more than one pair of each species other than the sociable house sparrow and house martin.

FILM YOUR GUESTS?

It is tempting to peer into nest-boxes to see what is going on, but you should not do this on any count. Disturbing nesting birds is illegal. If you want to give yourself and your family a real treat, lash out on a nest-box fitted with a tiny video camera that you can connect to your television set. Then you can sit back and watch your guests any time you like from the comfort of your armchair.

nest-boxes and give them a good clean. Wear gloves for this job because the boxes will inevitably contain fleas. If you put some soft wood-shavings or corrugated cardboard in the boxes after cleaning, birds may use them as winter roosts.

BUILDING SUPPLIES

However nice your nest-boxes might be, the birds still need to furnish them. You can help here by providing a variety of nesting materials, such as wool (not brightly coloured), feathers, hair from your hairdresser's floor,

Above: This blue tit is carrying a beakful of dog hair back to its nest, where it will be cleverly interwoven with feathers and other materials to make a soft and comfortable bed for the eggs and nestlings when they eventually hatch.

SPREAD THEM OUT

Most birds are territorial in the breeding season (see page 10), thus ensuring that each pair can find enough food for their offspring. So don't put up lots of similar boxes in a small area. A small garden is not likely to

Above: Dinner time: an exciting picture of nestling great tits being fed provided by a concealed nest-box camera.

BUILD YOUR BIRDS A HOME

If you are reasonably handy with a saw you can very easily make a nest-box suitable for tits and other small birds. All you need are a plank of wood 15cm wide and about 140cm long, together with a few nails or screws or some glue. The plank can be either rough or smooth and it should be about 18mm thick.

Cut it into lengths as shown in the diagram, and then give each piece a coat of non-toxic paint or varnish, paying particular attention to the cut surfaces. Avoid using creosote-like wood preservatives that can be harmful to birds. Contrary to popular opinion, the colour does not seem to matter to the birds. Recent surveys have shown that many birds will happily use brightly coloured boxes as long as they are properly situated.

The entrance hole can be at the front or on either side, but you obviously want it to be where you can watch the birds' comings and goings, so decide where you want to put your nest-box before making the hole and fitting the pieces together. If you opt for a front entrance, try to make the roof long enough to give a good overhang, so that rainwater is thrown well clear of the entrance.

You can nail or screw the box together, or glue the pieces together with a good waterproof wood glue. The hinge can be made from a strip of thick polythene or leather, or from a section of an old cycle inner tube. Fix the completed box in position with a couple of stout nails or corrosion-resistant screws secured through the back board.

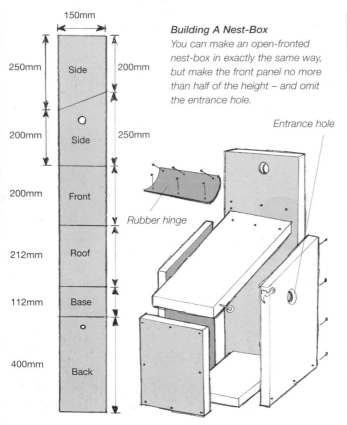

Building A Nest-Box
You can make an open-fronted nest-box in exactly the same way, but make the front panel no more than half of the height – and omit the entrance hole.

Entrance hole

Rubber hinge

150mm

250mm	Side	200mm
200mm	Side	250mm
200mm	Front	
212mm	Roof	
112mm	Base	
400mm	Back	

Above: *Don't expect new nest-boxes to be occupied straight away. Birds are wary of new things and take a while to accept them. This blue tit is inspecting a new box carefully and will examine it both inside and out before deciding to nest in it – or not!*

GET YOUR ENTRANCE RIGHT

The diameter of the entrance hole obviously determines which birds can use your nest-box, and you must get it right. If you are hoping to encourage blue tits and great tits, the entrance must be no more than 28mm across. Make it any larger than this and you will probably find house sparrows in residence. Nuthatches and redstarts can squeeze through a 35mm hole, while if you make the entrance 50mm or more the starlings will probably take an interest.

HOMES FOR HOUSE MARTINS

House martins usually fix their mud nests under the eaves of buildings and, although many people think these nests are unsightly, the birds themselves are delightful and well worth encouraging. Artificial nests can be made with sawdust and cement and providing such nests is a good way to attract the birds to areas where there is a lack of mud.

Moisten some fine sawdust with washing-up liquid and then mix it with dry cement in the ratio of three parts of sawdust to one of cement. Add enough water to make a mouldable paste. An up-turned plastic basin about 15cm in diameter can be used as a mould. Smear the outside with washing-up liquid and then

Above: A house martin feeding its young, which have been reared in an artificial martin box tucked safely under the eaves.

cover it with a layer of the cement mixture about 10-15mm thick. Don't make it too smooth, for the idea is to make it as much like a real nest as possible. When the cement is completely dry, remove the basin and use a fine saw to cut the cement cup vertically in half. This will give you two artificial nests. Carefully cut a semi-

circle about 28mm diameter from the outer rim – any more and the sparrows will move in – and glue the nest tight up under the eaves of your house. It may be easier to glue the nest to a piece of wood first, and then fix the wood to the wall. Martins are quite sociable birds, so you can put two or more nests close together, but don't expect immediate results.

Swallows also build with mud, but usually inside buildings. If you have a barn or open garage it is worth providing artificial nests. Shallow mud basins made in the same way as the martin nests (but not cut in half) can be fixed to rafters, or if there is a natural source of mud nearby, a simple platform may encourage the birds to move in.

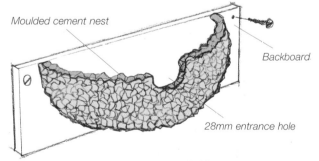

Moulded cement nest

Backboard

28mm entrance hole

Above: Cement/sawdust martin boxes are best glued to a piece of wood before being fixed under the eaves. Use a really strong glue!

HEALTH AND SAFETY

Once you start to encourage birds into your garden it is necessary to be aware of the dangers that they may face and to be prepared to minimize them in order to keep your visitors healthy and safe. Most of the precautions that you can take are very simple.

CATS

Cats are thought to kill over 50 million birds in Britain every year! If you have a cat of your own, give it a collar with a bell attached. This will warn the birds of the cat's approach. If other cats are a problem,

Above: *Early warning! Even the best-behaved cat finds it difficult to resist birds. A small bell on your pet's collar will warn the birds of approaching danger.*

you could try planting some prickly roses around the base of your bird-table, or perhaps surround it with a fence camouflaged with attractive plants. Ground-feeding is obviously a non-starter if you have problems with cats. Bird-tables and other feeders should also be sited fairly close to hedges or shrubs so that the birds can dive for cover if they are alarmed – by a sparrowhawk for example.

CLEAN UP REGULARLY

Stale food stuck around the edges of tables and other feeders can be a breeding ground for germs, so it is essential to keep the feeders clean. Brush them well with a mild disinfectant at least once a week. The birds' own droppings can also build up on a bird-table and cause problems. Never erect your bird-table under a tree where it may receive droppings from birds perched on the branches. Nest-boxes must also be thor-

oughly cleaned at the end of the season. The adult birds are very good at removing the babies' droppings, but they inevitably miss some and then old nest materials can become thoroughly impregnated with faeces and dropped food. There will also be plenty of fleas, waiting patiently in the pupal stage for the next year's birds to take up residence.

DON'T FORGET THE WATER

Although many birds, especially the insectivorous species, get a lot of water from their food, most of them need to drink several times a day. Most birds also enjoy a daily bath, which helps to keep them clean and free from various parasites. If you have a garden pond, try to have a shallow area where the birds can bathe and drink safely. If you have no pond, give your guests a bird bath. An ornamental bath can be an

Above: *Greenfinches are often seen on bird tables, but a group like this leaves droppings – so clean up before adding food.*

attractive garden feature, but the birds won't mind if you provide nothing more than an up-turned dustbin lid as long as you keep it topped up. And don't forget to keep it ice-free in the winter.

Above: Sparrows and other garden birds enjoy a good bath, even in the winter.

NO SALT

Salt is harmful to our garden birds as it interferes with the way in which they use the water in their bodies. Never give them salted peanuts or crisps, or any other salty foods. Even highly salted bacon rind can upset them.

BE CAREFUL WITH SLUG PELLETS

If you have to use poisons to protect your garden plants from slugs and snails, bear your birds in mind. Blue pellets are less likely to interest the birds than those with natural colours, but it still makes sense to cover them with lengths of wire netting to prevent the birds from pecking the dead slugs and picking up the poison that way. Mineral flakes and pellets that kill the pests by inflicting physical damage are much safer than poisons.

ACCIDENTS

Although birds are pretty good at avoiding obstacles in general, large windows may cause them problems. A bird flying towards the window may see nothing but the reflection of your garden, and then ... bang. Even a small bird can produce quite a clatter if it crashes into a window. The bird itself may only be stunned, and it may come round in a few minutes if you pick it up gently and wrap it in a warm cloth. Quite often, however, the neck is broken, and then there is nothing that you can do. The same goes for small birds that have been badly injured by cats.

You can reduce window collisions quite considerably by sticking silhouettes of hawks on the panes. The birds will see these and take avoiding action.

BABY BIRDS

Many young birds fall to the ground because they don't quite get the hang of flying on their first outing. Although it is tempting to 'rescue' them, the best thing is to lock up your cat and leave the baby birds where they are. The parent birds will probably be close at hand and, as long as the babies are not injured, they will help them to safety.

Nestlings that fall from their nests before they are properly developed are unlikely to survive for more than an hour or two. If you find such a casualty and know where it came from you could try putting it back in its nest, as long as you don't disturb the other occupants. Its chances will be slim, but at least you will have given it a chance.

Above: Baby robins are safe in their nest but few of them will survive in the outside world.

The laws of nature dictate that only one or two chicks from each brood will reach adulthood, so don't let these casualties distress you. With your continued help, the species will survive and there will always be another generation to entertain you the following year.

THE BIRDS' YEAR

Most of our garden birds are resident species that stay with us throughout the year. A number of other species, such as swallows and house martins, are summer visitors from Africa, and we also get winter visitors, such as the fieldfare and redwing, from northern Europe. The resident species and summer visitors may breed in our gardens, but the winter visitors do not.

Above: The wren's loud, warbling song is often delivered from a high branch and can be heard throughout the year.

SPRING

This is the start of the year for our birds, when their activities are focused on rearing a new generation. The males establish territories, and many of them become more brightly coloured at this time. They defend their territories against other males by singing (see page 10) and their songs also attract mates. Territory sizes vary according to the habitat, but are always big enough to provide enough food to feed a family. Nests are built by one or both birds before the female settles down to egg-laying. The birds need a lot of food at this stage, so you can help by always keeping the bird-table well-stocked.

SUMMER

Some birds continue to rear families well into the summer, with two or even three broods, but activity generally dies down in the summer months. Territories are abandoned and bird song is much less evident. This is the time when many birds moult, with young birds getting their adult plumage and adults replacing worn-out feathers.

The males commonly lose their breeding colours when they moult. Moulting birds often cannot fly and they hide away in the vegetation for safety.

AUTUMN

The summer visitors fly off to Africa, often congregating in large numbers on trees or tele-phone wires beforehand as if

Above: Redwings arrive as winter approaches and they enjoy our fallen apples.
Below: These baby great tits continue to demand food long after they have left the nest.

Above: A roof on your bird table will keep off much of the snow and rain, but it is not strictly necessary.

waiting for the signal to leave. The winter visitors start to arrive soon afterwards. These migrations are triggered by changes in day length. The birds do not wait until the weather gets cold or food gets short – this could be too late.

WINTER

Birds have to work especially hard during the short days of winter to find enough food to see them through the long and often very cold nights. With the notable exception of the robin, few birds bother about territories at this time of year: they flock together in places where they can find the most food. Extra food on the bird-table can be a real life-saver at this time of year because the birds will not have to spend a lot of time and energy searching for it. Energy-rich fatty foods are especially valuable in the winter.

CALLS AND SONGS

The wide range of sounds made by birds can be roughly divided into calls and songs. Calls are relatively short notes, sometimes repeated two or three times, and they are used mainly to warn other birds of danger or to keep in contact with mates or young. They are relatively easy to 'translate' into human sounds, although not everyone interprets them into the same way. Songs are much more complex outpourings of sound, used mainly to defend territories and to attract mates in the early spring. Few attempts have been made to 'translate' them in this book.

YOUR MONTHLY CHECKLIST

January Ensure the bird-bath remains ice-free by pouring hot water on it when necessary.

February Make sure any new nest-boxes are in position by the middle of the month.

March The nesting season is under way: provide nesting materials as well as plenty of food.

April Watch out for the arrival of swallows, house martins, and other summer visitors.

May Nesting birds will appreciate a few mealworms which they can take back to their chicks.

June Natural food is plentiful, so you can reduce the amount of food given, but do not stop feeding altogether.

July Keep the bird-bath topped up: the water evaporates rapidly in hot weather.

August This is a fairly quiet month for garden birds – a good time to check your feeders and give them a good clean.

September The nesting season is over, so you can trim your shrubs and hedges without risk of disturbing the birds.

October Clean out all your nest-boxes and carry out any necessary repairs.

November Increase the amounts of food that you provide now that the cold weather has arrived.

December The winter visitors have arrived, so scatter apples on your lawn for fieldfares and redwings.

HOUSE SPARROW

Passer domesticus

Although less common than they once were, these sociable birds feed in nearly every garden and they stay with us throughout the year. Both sexes have grey cheeks and a brown back with conspicuous black stripes. The male also has a black bib. There is not much of a song, but the variety of cheerful chirps is not unpleasant to listen to.

FOOD

The sturdy beak shows that the house sparrow is basically a seed-eater, although it will eat almost anything you care to put out for it – bread, soft fruit, peanuts, fat, and all the commercial bird foods, including mealworms.

NESTING

House sparrows are rarely found far from human habitation, where they make untidy nests of grass, lined with hair and feathers and other soft materials. Creeper-clad walls are favourite spots for the nests, but the birds also build in holes and crevices and will happily make their way into your roof-space. Breeding starts in April, with three broods often being reared during spring and summer. The nests are also used for roosting in the winter. Several pairs usually nest close together, on neighbouring houses or even on a single house, and all the birds feed together, often moving from garden to garden during the day. Such a colony may remain in the same place for several years and then, for no apparent reason, abandon the site in favour of one else-

Above: House sparrows are about 15cm long. Only the male has the black bib and grey crown. Females and young are duller, with brown crowns. Although they can rip up crocus flowers, they are fun to watch and worth encouraging by providing food and nest-boxes.

where in the town or village. The birds rarely move more than a few hundred metres from their original homes.

Above: Fixed in a corner under the eaves, this simple open-ended nest box will accommodate a family of house sparrows.

A HELPING HAND

One of the reasons given for the bird's decline has been the lack of nooks and crannies in modern houses, so you can help by providing extra nest sites. The simplest is a tunnel made from two pieces of wood joined at right angles and fixed under the eaves. Put it in a corner if possible, otherwise simply block off one end. Provide some dried grass and some hair or wool and the birds will be very happy. The birds will also use standard open-fronted nest-boxes if these are concealed in vegetation.

DUNNOCK
Prunella modularis

With its streaky brown back, this common little bird is often mistaken for a sparrow, and is often called the hedge sparrow. But a look at its slender beak, designed mainly for a diet of insects, will show that it is not closely related to the sparrows. It is a resident species wherever there are sufficient bushes or other dense vegetation to give it the cover it requires. It is a shy bird, rarely moving far from shelter and darting for cover at the slightest disturbance. Dunnocks are much less sociable than house sparrows and are usually seen only in ones or twos in the garden, although larger numbers may feed together in the winter. The call is a fairly harsh, whistling *seep-seep-seep*, while the song is a rather rapid warble.

FOOD

Dunnocks feed mainly on insects and spiders, but also take fruit and small seeds in autumn and winter. They usually feed on or close to the ground and much of their food is found by foraging among dead leaves.

both fresh and dried mealworms. Nest-boxes hold no attraction for dunnocks, but the birds will appreciate a supply of hair or fine wool, and perhaps some feathers, with which to line their nests during the nesting season.

NESTING

The neat, cup-shaped nests are made from slender twigs interwoven with leaves and moss and lined with hair and feathers. They are normally built low down in shrubs and hedgerows or perhaps in dense creepers on a wall. Two or three broods are reared from April onwards.

A HELPING HAND

Although rarely seen on a traditional bird-table – it prefers to collect food falling to the ground below – the dunnock will readily come to a ground-station for small seeds. It also enjoys chopped dried fruit and

Above: *The dunnock is about 14cm long, with a steely grey head and neck and a brown patch around the eye. Juveniles have streaks on the neck and throat, but their general coloration is otherwise just like that of the adult birds.*

STARLING
Sturnus vulgaris

Although it may look completely black from a distance, the starling's glossy plumage has a metallic green and purple sheen and pale spots, the latter being especially noticeable in winter. The long, multi-purpose beak is yellow in summer and brown in winter. Starlings are resident almost everywhere, including city centres, and they are among the commonest of British birds. They are gregarious creatures, forming huge winter roosting flocks that often damage trees and buildings with their droppings. Smaller groups scour our gardens for food, and in the spring and summer these are usually family groups, with the parents feeding perhaps half a dozen youngsters. The latter are dull brown and resemble female blackbirds, but starlings are easily recognized by their strutting walk, quite different from the hopping movements of most other garden birds. There is a wide vocabulary of warbling and whistling calls, commonly delivered from roof-tops and often mimicking the calls of other birds.

FOOD
Starlings are omnivorous birds and will eat almost anything, but fruit and insects form the bulk of their natural diet. They frequently damage crops of cherries and soft fruit.

NESTING
The nest is an untidy pile of straw and leaves, lined with moss and feathers. It is usually built in a hole in a tree or building, although it is some-times wedged among dense creepers on a wall. Several pairs may nest in close prox-imity. One or two broods are reared from late March onwards.

A HELPING HAND
Starlings will eat almost anything you care to give them, on the ground or on the bird-table. Although some bird-watchers accuse them of being 'bullies' and chasing the smaller birds away, they can be great fun to watch, especially when they try to get food from hanging feeders – they are not very good at this! They are particularly appreciative of apples scattered on the lawn in the winter and, although they might squabble over choice morsels, they usually feed happily with the blackbirds at this time. Starlings will use well-concealed open-fronted nest-boxes, and also enclosed boxes as long as the entrance hole is at least 5cm in diameter.

Above and below: The starling is about 22cm long. It flies rapidly, and in flight its wings reveal their triangular outline.

BLACKBIRD

Turdus merula

The adult male blackbird, true to its name, is jet black, with a bright yellow beak and a yellow ring around each eye. No other garden bird looks like this. The female, however, is sooty brown, with a brown beak and a streaky breast. Juveniles are also brown and very spotty. Blackbirds are with us throughout the year, living wherever there are trees and shrubs in which to nest and open ground on which to feed. They can be seen in nearly every garden. They are not particularly sociable and, although several may feed together in winter, one may suddenly dart at another and see it off. The birds run or hop, but never strut like the starling. The rich, whistling or flute-like song can be heard throughout the breeding season, while the loud *chink-chink-chink*, which alerts all the other garden birds, is uttered whenever the blackbird senses danger.

FOOD

Blackbirds are not fussy eaters and exist on a wide range of plant and animal foods. They are especially fond of blackberries and elderberries in late summer, when their purple droppings can be seen all over the hedgerows. They also enjoy red currants in the garden. Animal food includes insects and spiders, and every gardener knows that they are very fond of earthworms. Quick to explore any area of recently dug soil, they can also detect worms under the lawn – cocking the head from side to side as they listen for the slightest sound, and then plunging in the beak to begin what is often a fascinating tug-of-war with the worm.

NESTING

The cup-shaped nest is built in a thick hedge or other dense vegetation. It is made largely with dry grass and thin twigs, lined with mud, and then provided with an inner lining of fine plant material. Two or three broods are reared from April onwards.

A HELPING HAND

Blackbirds will eat almost anything that you care to offer in the way of fat, cheese, biscuit crumbs, soft seeds, and dried fruit. They will come to the bird-table, but they prefer a ground-feeding station. Apples are much appreciated in winter. Newspapers often carry amusing pictures of blackbird nests built in odd places, such as bicycle baskets and saddle-bags, but the birds prefer natural sites and even open-fronted nest-boxes are rarely used if natural sites are available.

Above: Blackbirds are 20-30cm long and the tail is much longer than that of the starling. An immature male has a dark bill and a much duller eye-ring than the adult pictured here.

SONG THRUSH
Turdus philomelos

The brown back and the triangular spots on the buff or sandy-coloured breast distinguish this fine songster. The clear, flute-like song consists of several distinct phrases, each repeated two, three, or four times. When alarmed, the birds utter a high-pitched *cheek-cheek-cheek*, although the commonest call is a softer *sip-sip-sip*. Song thrushes are strongly territorial and you will rarely see more than one or two at a time in the garden. As a resident species, the bird remains with us all the year, but its numbers have fallen dramatically in recent years and it has disappeared from many gardens.

Left: The song thrush is about 22cm long and the sexes are alike. In flight the song thrush reveals a pale brown patch under the wing, although this is not always easy to spot.

Below: Holding the snail shell firmly by the rim, the song thrush brings it sharply down on to a stone to break it open. No other bird has learned how to deal with snails in this way.

NESTING
Song thrushes like to nest in thick hedgerows and other dense vegetation and may start building as early as March. The cup-shaped nest is built with an assortment of dry vegetation, including moss and dead leaves, and smoothly plastered inside with a mix of mud and rotten wood. Three broods may be reared during the next three or four months.

FOOD
Song thrushes eat a wide range of insects, spiders, worms, and other small creatures, but their favourite foods are snails. The first indication that a song thrush is about is often a loud tapping sound, produced as the bird hammers a snail shell against a stone 'anvil'. This goes on until the shell shatters and the bird can hook out the soft body. The bird also appreciates the fruit-laden hedges and shrubberies in autumn.

A HELPING HAND
Song thrushes can be attracted with a 'soft-bill' mix containing sultanas and other dried fruit and cheese, best offered on a ground station. The birds also enjoy living and dried mealworms. If you don't have a rockery or a concrete path, try placing a few large stones or pieces of paving around the garden for the birds to use as anvils. The carpet of broken shells around a regular anvil will show you just how well the song thrush keeps your snail population under control – for free and without poisons. Song thrushes are not very interested in nes boxes, but may build in open-fronted boxes hidden in ivy or other creepers on a wall. A bag of dried grass and other natural nesting materials may encourage them to settle down in your garden.

ROBIN
Erithacus rubecula

Everyone knows and loves the cheerful robin – so much so that it has been adopted as our national bird. It is common in most habitats with trees and bushes, but it is very territorial and, unless the male is feeding his mate, you are unlikely to see more than one robin at a time. Both sexes hold territories for much of the year. Each territory covers perhaps half an acre, and if another adult robin dares to enter it the owner merely has to puff up his or her red breast in a display of aggression to frighten the intruder away. Dunnocks and other small birds may also be chased away. The song, a very musical medley of *triddle-eee-triddle-ooo-triddle-eee*, is usually delivered from a tree or the top of a hedge and, unlike that of other garden birds, it can be heard throughout the winter. The birds also utter a loud alarm call – *tic-tic-tic* – repeated rapidly and sounding rather like an angler's reel as the line unwinds.

Above: The robin is about 13cm long. Young robins have speckled plumage without any red. This prevents adults from attacking them.

and female pool their territories and each female settles down to build a nest. The latter is usually constructed in a hole in a tree or a wall, but sometimes wedged into dense creepers. It is made with grass, moss, and leaves and lined with hair and wool. Two or three broods are reared during the spring and summer.

A HELPING HAND

Cheese, cake crumbs, fat, soft seeds, and dried fruit are all eagerly taken from the bird-table, but the undoubted favourite is the mealworm. Robins will do almost anything for mealworms! Scatter a few on the ground or the bird-table when a robin is about and it will very soon find them, and after a few days it will happily take them from your hand. Open-fronted nest-boxes may be used if they are well-concealed. Provide some hair or wool for extra encouragement.

FOOD

The robin's slender beak indicates a natural diet consisting mainly of insects and spiders, many of which are collected on the lawn or unearthed among fallen leaves and other debris. Earthworms also figure largely on the robin's menu and the bird is never far away when we are digging our gardens. Fruits and soft seeds become important in autumn and winter.

NESTING

Towards the end of the winter the females begin intruding into the males' territories, and the males begin to tolerate their presence. Eventually a male

CHAFFINCH
Fringilla coelebs

The male chaffinch can be recognized by its pink breast and blue-grey crown combined with its two white wing bars. Females and juveniles lack the pink and blue and have narrower wing bars. Resident wherever there are trees and bushes in which to nest, it accounts for up to 40 per cent of the bird population in deciduous woodlands and there can be few gardens without chaffinches in the winter. After the wren, the chaffinch is probably Britain's commonest breeding bird. The birds are strongly territorial during the breeding season but form loose flocks at other times and you may well see half a dozen or more in the garden. Larger flocks seen in the fields in the winter consist mainly of visitors from northern Europe. The chaffinch has a powerful, musical voice and a varied repertoire of songs, including the familiar *ship-ship-ship-shooee-sheerio*, which always ends flourishing crescendo. It also has a wide vocabulary of calls, the commonest of which is *pink-pink*, uttered mainly when perched.

Below: The chaffinch is about 15cm long. The male is easily recognized, although less colourful in winter. The female's white wing bars (right) distinguish her from the female house sparrow.

FOOD
Both adults and young exist almost entirely on caterpillars and other insects during the breeding season, but seeds, including large quantities of beech nuts, make up most of the diet at other times. The birds nearly always feed on the ground.

NESTING
The chaffinch builds a neat cup-shaped nest in the fork of a branch. Grass and moss are the main constituents, with a lining of hair and feathers and an outer covering of lichen bound on with spider silk. There is usually just one brood.

A HELPING HAND
Chaffinches happily take bird-pudding, small seeds, and mealworms from a ground-feeding station. They are not great ones for eating from the traditional bird-table and are more likely to forage under-neath it for scraps scattered other birds. They are not inter-ested in nest-boxes, although they may appreciate a supply of wool or hair that can be used for lining their nests.

BULLFINCH
Pyrrhula pyrrhula

Fruit growers are not keen on seeing this chunky bird in their gardens because it gorges itself on the buds of trees and bushes in the spring. It is much less common now than it was a few years ago, however, and bird-gardeners are usually very happy to see it. The male has a deep pink breast, a black cap, and a white rump and cannot really be confused with any other bird. The female has the black cap and white rump, but is otherwise a much duller bird. The bullfinch is resident in woods and hedgerows as well as orchards and mature gardens all over the British Isles. It is a fairly quiet bird, its main call being a rather melancholy whistle – *peeoo-peeoo-peeoo*.

FOOD

The bullfinch is one of the few small birds to specialize in buds. These may contribute as much as a third of its annual food consumption. It peels off the outer scales with its sharp-edged beak and swallows the inner leaves. As well as buds, the bullfinch eats insects and spiders and a wide range of seeds.

Ripening ash keys are a particular favourite in autumn and winter. These and other fruits are almost always taken directly from the trees, for the bullfinch rarely comes to the ground.

NESTING

Bullfinches mate for life and, except when the female is sitting on the nest, they are nearly always seen in pairs, although several pairs may roam the countryside together in autumn and winter. The nest is usually built in a dense shrub, often an evergreen, and consists of a loose cup of moss and twigs lined with hair and fine roots. Two or three broods are reared from April onwards.

A HELPING HAND

The birds may visit the bird-table in hard weather if fruits and small seeds are offered, but they prefer to stay in the bushes. They are not interested in nest-boxes. Plant a variety of shrubs for them, and if they like your garden they will visit you.

Left: The bullfinch is about 17cm long. Youngsters have the black wings but otherwise are largely brown. The white rump can be seen from above and below when the bird is in flight. Look also for the prominent white wing bar.

GREENFINCH
Carduelis chloris

This fairly sociable bird can be found wherever there are trees and bushes in which it can nest, but it is most abundant on the edges of woodland, especially where these are close to farmland on which it likes to feed in the winter. It is one of the commonest visitors to the garden in the winter, when half a dozen or more can often be seen queuing up to take their turns at the bird-table. It is easily distinguished from the superficially similar sparrows by the yellow edges to the wings and tail. The rest of the body is greenish brown, although the male becomes much greener in the summer. Its most distinctive call, uttered mainly by the male, is a repetitive *chup-chup-chup*. There is also a somewhat wheezy song – *shwee-shwee-shwee* – usually delivered from a prominent perch.

FOOD
Greenfinches feed mainly on fruits and seeds, especially those of low-growing plants. Large flocks sometimes gather to feed in the fields in the winter. The birds also take buds from trees and shrubs in the spring.

NESTING
Greenfinches normally nest in dense shrubs, especially ever-greens, and several pairs may build quite close together. The nest is a bulky cup made from twigs, grass, and moss, and lined with fine roots and hair. Two broods are normally reared from late April onwards.

A HELPING HAND
Although in the wild they feed mainly on the ground, green-finches are perfectly happy to dine at the bird-table and will eat almost any starchy food that you care to provide. They are particularly fond of peanuts and sunflower seeds, and these are best offered in hanging feeders where the birds can display their agility as well as their yellow wing and tail flashes. Greenfinches are unimpressed by nest-boxes, but you can encourage them to settle in your garden by planting evergreen shrubs. They enjoy the cover provided by the fast-growing *leylandii* trees, but this is not a good idea! They grow far too tall for the average garden and often engender disputes with neigh-bours. Holly is a better choice

Above: *The greenfinch is about 15cm long. Females and winter males are much browner than the summer males pictured here. Juveniles are greyish brown with dark streaks above and below. The yellow wing bars are present at all stages.*

GOLDFINCH
Carduelis carduelis

This delightful little bird is easy to recognize by its red face, white collar, and broad yellow wing-bar. A resident species, it visits our gardens mainly in autumn and winter, usually in small groups appropriately known as charms. It is one of the few birds in the United Kingdom that seem to be increasing their numbers. A recent survey by the British Trust for Ornithology found that it was visiting more than half of our gardens, whereas ten years ago it was seen in less than a quarter of the gardens surveyed. The commonest call is a cheerful *switt-switt-switt* or *swillitt-swillitt-swillitt*.

FOOD

Goldfinches are essentially birds of open country, including farmland, where they can find the small seeds that form the bulk of their food. They are not keen on feeding on the ground and can often be seen attacking the seed-heads of thistles, dandelions, and other members of the daisy family, using their wings to balance as they tug out the seeds. Because their beaks are fairly dainty, they prefer soft seeds and frequently pull the flower-heads to bits long before the seeds are ripe. The birds also eat plenty of small insects, especially in the spring.

Above: *The goldfinch is about 13cm long. Its recent increase in numbers is undoubtedly due to the increasing provision of suitable food by gardeners.*

NESTING

Goldfinches nest mainly in trees and tall shrubs, often on the finer branches that seem hardly strong enough to support them. The cup-shaped nests are built with moss and lichen and lined with wool and hair and even spider silk. There are generally two broods, reared from early May onwards.

A HELPING HAND

A patch of thistles and teasels will certainly attract goldfinches to your garden, and do try to leave a patch of dandelions at the base of a wall or hedge. If you are not keen on these plants you can grow Michaelmas daisies instead. The birds will also take small or crushed seeds from your bird-table and other feeders, but for a real treat given them niger seeds. Goldfinches can't resist these tiny, black, oil-rich seeds and have an uncanny ability to home in on them as soon as they are hung out in the garden – but you do need a special feeder for these seeds, otherwise they will blow away in the slightest breeze (see page 15). Although nest-boxes do not interest goldfinches, they will appreciate bags of moss and bits of wool – or hair from the hair-dresser's floor – when they start to build their nests.

BLUE TIT
Parus caeruleus

Easily recognized by its bright blue crown, black eyestripe, and yellow breast, the lively little blue tit is one of our commonest and most popular garden birds. It is present in nearly every garden, especially in the winter, and surveys conducted by the RSPB have shown that the numbers visiting our gardens have increased significantly in recent years – undoubtedly as a result of feeding. The bird is resident wherever there are trees. Large numbers gather to feed in the winter and, although you may not see more than half a dozen or so at one time in your garden, the birds are always on the move and dozens or even hundreds may pass through the garden in a day, staying just long enough to refuel at your feeding station. The rather squeaky song, which can be heard for much of the year, consists of variations on a theme of *tsee-tsee-tsee-tu-tu-tu*, often finishing with a marked flourish during the breeding season.

FOOD

Insects, especially caterpillars, form the bulk of the blue tit's diet in spring and summer, and the birds perform amazing acrobatics as they pluck them from the slenderest of twigs. They also eat spiders and lots of aphids, and also take nectar and pollen from flowers. In autumn and winter they scour the tree trunks and branches for aphid eggs, although small seeds are their main foods at this time.

Below: The blue tit is about 11cm long. Females are less brightly coloured than the male, pictured here.

NESTING

Blue tits usually breed in holes in trees, where they build cup-shaped nests with moss and grass. The nests are usually lined with feathers and hair and the female lays her eggs in April or May.

A HELPING HAND

Blue tits will eat most foods that you offer, but are particularly fond of fatty offerings and peanuts. They display great agility and ingenuity when extracting the nuts from various feeders and, despite their tiny beaks, they can deal with quite large nuts – taking them off to a branch and hammering them to pieces while holding them down with the feet. But don't offer large nuts in the breeding season. The birds readily adopt enclosed nest-boxes fixed to walls or tree trunks, even in quite exposed situations, but if you want to keep out sparrows the entrance hole must be no more than 28mm in diameter.

GREAT TIT

Parus major

Great tits are resident wherever there are trees and commonly mingle with blue tits in the garden throughout the year. The two species are often confused, although the great tit is a little larger than the blue tit and readily distinguished by its black crown and the bold black stripe on its bright yellow belly. The bird has a wide repertoire of calls and songs, the best known of which is the rather harsh whistling *teacher-teacher-teacher*. This often resembles the sound of a bicycle pump in action and in some places the bird is jokingly known as the bicycle bird. Another common call is *tink-tink-tink*, which can easily be confused with the call of the chaffinch.

FOOD

Like the blue tit, the great tit feeds mainly on caterpillars and other insects in the breeding season and on various fruits and seeds at other times. It also eats buds in the spring. Beech nuts are a favourite food in the autumn, when large flocks gather to feed in the woods. The nuts are crushed in the beak or hammered to pieces underfoot.

NESTING

Great tits start to pair up and set up territories in late winter, and are then most often seen in pairs. They nest in holes in trees, rocks, or walls, building a cup with moss and other vegetation and lining it largely with hair or wool. The birds occasionally build within the old nest of another bird, as long as it is well concealed. The eggs are usually laid in April.

A HELPING HAND

Peanuts, sunflower seeds, cheese, and suet or bird-pudding will bring plenty of great tits to your garden in the winter. An enclosed nest-box may encourage a pair to settle down and breed. Although larger than the blue tit, the birds will squeeze through an entrance hole only 28mm across – small enough to exclude house sparrows.

Right: *The great tit can be quite aggressive and regularly ousts its smaller blue tit cousins from garden feeding stations.*

Above: *At about 14cm long, the great tit is the largest of our tits. The sexes are alike, although the male has a wider and more sharply defined black stripe on the underside.*

COAL TIT

Parus ater

True to its name, the coal tit is a somewhat 'dirty' version of the great tit. It is certainly less colourful, with a black crown, steely-grey back, and a dirty white or buff underside. It is also smaller than the great tit, but the most obvious feature is the white patch on the back of the head. The coal tit is a common woodland resident, especially in coniferous woodlands, and a regular visitor to many bird-tables in the winter.

Although still less common in the garden than the blue tit and great tit, it has shown a marked increase in recent years – undoubtedly due to the increased popularity of coniferous trees and shrubs. The song, which can be heard for much of the year, is a higher-pitched version of the great tit's *tea<u>cher</u>-tea<u>cher</u>-tea<u>cher</u>,* while the commonest call is a rather sad *teeoo-teeoo-teeoo,* falling in pitch towards the end.

FOOD

In common with our other tits, the coal tit feeds on insects – especially aphids – spiders, and seeds. The insects and spiders are gathered mainly from coniferous trees, while the seeds are taken mainly from the ground.

extract food from all the usual hanging feeders. Although it sometimes uses nest-boxes, it is less enthusiastic about them than the blue tit.

Right and below: The coal tit is about 12cm long. The two white wing bars and the white patch at the back of the head distinguish it from the great tit.

NESTING

Coal tits nest in holes, usually fairly close to the ground and sometimes in the ground itself. The nest is a cup, made largely of moss, often bound with spider silk, and lined with a thick layer of hair and feathers. Eggs are laid from May onwards and each pair normally rears two broods of young in a year.

A HELPING HAND

The coal tit particularly enjoys cheese and other fatty foods, but will take all the usual foods found on the bird-table, including peanuts and a wide range of other seeds. It is just as agile as the blue tit and can

LONG-TAILED TIT

Aegithalos caudatus

The long tail, accounting for more than half of the total length, makes this dainty and incredibly agile little bird easy to recognize. The head is largely white, with a broad black band above the eye, and the shoulders are chestnut brown. The underside is white with a variable pink tinge. Young birds lack the pink tinge below. Long-tailed tits are resident birds, living mainly in wooded areas with plenty of undergrowth and also on heathland. They are sociable birds and for most of the year they travel around in small flocks. They are most likely to be seen in the garden in the winter, when a flock may arrive and scour the trees and shrubs for an hour or two before moving on. Their constant, squeaky twittering – *see-see-see* – keeps the flock together and the sound is often the first indication of their presence.

FOOD

Long-tailed tits feed mainly on insects and spiders, which they find almost entirely in the trees and bushes. They also eat soft fruit and small seeds but their tiny beaks cannot deal with anything very hard.

NESTING

Unlike our other tits, the long-tailed tit does not nest in holes. It usually builds in dense shrubs – sometimes on ivy-covered walls – and the nest is a compact oval ball of moss and lichen, bound together with hair and spider silk and thickly lined with feathers. Close to human habitation, a nest may also include scraps of paper and plastic. The birds enter through a small hole near the top and the female lays her eggs from late March onwards.

A HELPING HAND

Long-tailed tits have become more common in gardens in recent years and, although they keep mainly to the trees and hedges, they will come to

Above and left: *The long-tailed tit is about 15cm long and has a rather fluffy appearance.*

feeding stations in cold weather. Bird-pudding (see p. 13), cheese, and suet will encourage them, and they will also display their agility while chipping away at peanuts in a variety of feeders. Although they have no interest in nest-boxes, they may well nest in gardens with dense hedges or shrubberies.

WREN

Troglodytes troglodytes

The wren is a tiny, rounded bird with finely barred brown plumage and a short tail that is often held almost vertically. It is Britain's commonest breeding bird, living in woodland with plenty of thick undergrowth and almost everywhere else with dense vegetation. Few gardens are without it, although it is less often seen than other birds because it usually keeps under cover. When spotted scampering through the herbaceous garden or the hedge bottom, it is commonly mistaken for a mouse! The wren might not be easy to see, but you can't fail to hear it: for such a small bird it has a remarkably loud voice. Its song, which can be heard throughout the year, is a high-pitched metallic warble – *svee-svee-svee-seeeee* – lasting for about five seconds and finishing with a real flourish. There is also a shrill alarm call – *tic-tic-tic*.

Above and right: *The wren is about 9cm long. Although wrens are strongly territorial for much of the year, they become quite sociable in the winter and often roost together to keep warm.*

FOOD

Wrens feed almost entirely on insects and spiders, plucked from the ground and from bark crevices with the slender beak.

NESTING

At the start of the breeding season, usually some time in April, the male wren sets to work to build several nests in his territory. They are usually built in some sort of hole or crevice, often in a wall, or wedged among dense creepers. Constructed with grass, moss, and other vegetation, each nest is a hollow ball. The female then chooses one, lines it with feathers, and lays her eggs in it. Some males manage to persuade two or even three females to move into their nests – and then they really have to work hard to feed the families.

A HELPING HAND

Because wrens prefer to feed on the ground, they rarely visit the bird-table, although they will take meal-worms and biscuit crumbs from a ground-station. A good way to encourage the birds into your garden is to build a log-pile (see p. 9) that will harbour plenty of creepy-crawlies for them and also give them somewhere to hide their nests. If you have an old wall, try removing a stone or brick: wrens might well build in the gap, especially if it is protected by ivy or other vegetation. The birds rarely breed in nest-boxes, but they often roost in them during the winter, when a dozen or more can sometimes be found keeping warm in a single box.

TREECREEPER

Certhia familiaris

The spotty brown back and wings resemble those of the house sparrow and the dunnock, but the pure white underside and slender, downwardly curved beak immediately distinguish this agile little bird. A resident species, it is most common in mixed woodland, especially those with plenty of oaks, but it also frequents tree-lined avenues, parks, orchards, and gardens with mature trees. It utters its high-pitched *tsee-tsee-tsee* in flight and also while foraging on the tree trunks.

FOOD

The treecreeper feeds entirely on insects and spiders, which it plucks from bark crevices as it scurries up the tree trunks and larger branches. Having reached the top of a trunk, it

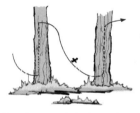

flies down and starts again on a neighbouring tree. Unlike the nuthatch, it cannot climb down the trunk. Aphid eggs form a significant part of its winter diet.

NESTING

Treecreepers normally nest under loose bark on tree trunks, but occasionally build in dense ivy clinging to trees and walls. The nest is built with moss, grass, and roots and lined with hair and feathers. Two broods are usually reared from April onwards.

A HELPING HAND

As a confirmed insectivore, the treecreeper is not likely to visit

the bird-table, but it may appreciate some dried meal-worms rammed into bark crevices, perhaps embedded in

*Above: The treecreeper's stiff tail feathers help to support the bird when it is feeding on vertical tree trunks. The birds sometimes search garden fences and shed walls for food.
Left: The treecreeper is about 12cm long and the sexes are similar in appearance.*

a bit of suet or bird-pudding. It readily takes to narrow wedge-shaped nest-boxes if these are fixed to tree trunks or among dense creepers, and it will appreciate a supply of wool, hair, moss, and feathers.

NUTHATCH
Sitta europaea

This sprightly little bird is easily identified by its blue-grey head and back, its rusty-orange sides, and the black stripe running through its eye. It lives mainly in woodlands, especially in oak-woods, but also frequents parks and gardens with mature trees. Although resident in most parts of England and Wales, it is absent from Ireland and most of Scotland. Its call is a loud and quite musical *chwit-chwit-chwit*, often delivered from a position high in a tree.

FOOD

Nuthatches eat a wide range of insects, spiders, and seeds. The insects and spiders are taken mainly from bark crevices and the bird can run both up and down a tree trunk as it searches – using its unusually long toes to maintain a grip on the bark. As the name suggests, it also eats nuts – acorns and hazel nuts are wedged into bark crevices and hammered open with the strong, pointed beak. Empty shells remain in the bark and if you find them you can be sure that nuthatches are about. The hammering sound, heard more often than the bird's call, carries for a considerable distance and can be confused with a woodpecker's drumming (see p. 46), although it is less rapid. The nuthatch is, in fact, often mistaken for a small woodpecker.

NESTING

The nest is always built in a hole, usually in a tree trunk, although wall cavities may also be used. The birds can reduce the size of the entrance hole by plastering it with mud if necessary. The nest itself is a simple cup made with leaves and flakes of bark. The eggs are laid in April or May.

A HELPING HAND

Nuthatches readily come to a bird-table offering nuts and seeds, but they are messy feeders and often scatter the food everywhere. They are also aggressive to other small birds. The best way to feed them is to offer hazel nuts wedged into bark crevices if you have suitable trees. Peanuts and shelled brazil nuts can be fixed into nut logs (see p. 17), while strings of peanuts in their shells allow the birds to show off their agility. The birds will use enclosed nest-boxes as long as the entrance is over 28mm in diameter.

Below: Nuthatches are about 14cm long. Males and females are alike, but juvenile birds only have a pale eye-stripe.

COLLARED DOVE

Streptopelia decaocto

Unknown in the British Isles until the 1950s this bird is now one of our commonest garden visitors, although its numbers have fallen slightly in recent years. It is easily recognized by the thin black collar and dark wing-tips on an otherwise fairly uniform pale grey plumage. Although resident all over lowland Britain, it dislikes wide open spaces and is particularly common in and around towns and villages. Its repetitive *coo-cooo-coo* call, in which the second syllable is the longest and often accented, is often delivered from roof-tops and chimneys and repeated with boring regularity. Some people confuse it with the call of the cuckoo, but the latter is much more musical and usually has just two syllables. The collared dove utters a single-syllable *coo* in flight.

FOOD

Collared doves are largely vegetarian and feed almost entirely on the ground. They eat some insects, especially in the spring, and attack berries in the autumn, but cereal grains and other seeds make up the bulk of their food throughout the year. They scour the fields for grain in the autumn.

NESTING

Collared doves are not the world's best nest-builders. They lay their eggs on platforms of twigs so flimsy that the eggs are clearly visible from below. These simple nests are usually constructed in trees, but occasionally on ledges on bridges and other buildings. Several broods, each with just two youngsters, may be reared from early spring through to around October.

A HELPING HAND

An assortment of seeds, including wheat or barley, presented on a ground-feeder or simply scattered on the lawn, will keep the collared doves happy. You will also see the birds under the bird-table and other feeders, mopping up the food scattered by the other birds. Nest-boxes do not interest them, although they may adopt large, open-fronted boxes or build on a simple platform wedged among the branches.

Above: Collared doves are about 33cm long and the sexes are alike. The distinctive white-tipped tail feathers are very prominent in flight. Because the breeding season lasts for about six months, the birds are commonly seen in pairs in spring and summer.

WOODPIGEON

Columba palumbus

This is Britain's largest and commonest pigeon, easily recognized by the white flash on each side of its neck and the rounded pink breast. Each wing is crossed by a white bar which is very prominent in flight. The bird is generally resident wherever there are trees for breeding, including gardens, town parks and cemeteries. Its persistent five-syllable cooing call – *coo-coo-coooo-cu-cu*, with the accent on the second or third syllable – is a familiar sound everywhere, as is the loud clatter of its wings when it takes off.

FOOD

Woodpigeons are essentially vegetarians, feeding on fruits and seeds and assorted vegetation. They are a nuisance on farmland, where large flocks gather and destroy huge areas of rape and other brassica crops as well as clover and cereals. They also take buds from many garden plants.

NESTING

The nest is little more than a platform of interwoven sticks fixed in a tree. The birds can breed at any time, but most youngsters are reared in late summer, when there is plenty of grain for them to eat. There are usually two or three broods, each consisting of just two chicks.

Above: Woodpigeons take fruits and buds from the trees, but feed mainly on the ground.
Left: Woodpigeons are about 40cm long. Juveniles lack the white neck flash.

A HELPING HAND

Woodpigeons do not really need any help from us, and most gardeners prefer to discourage them. But if you want to encourage them into your garden you need do nothing more than scatter some grain or slices of bread on your lawn.

TOWN PIGEON
Columba livia

Also known as feral pigeons, the pigeons that flock in nearly every town started out as rock doves living on mountains and coastal cliffs. Rock doves were domesticated many centuries ago and used for food, and were later adopted for sport and for carrying messages. Inevitably, many escaped from captivity, and these were the ancestors of today's town pigeons. The latter exist in an enormous range of colours, from the grey of the original rock dove to rusty brown, black, and even white, but they lack the white wing bars and neck flashes of the woodpigeon. Extremely sociable birds, they feed in large flocks wherever they can find food, and this includes farms, villages, factories, dockyards, and railway yards. They also roost communally. The birds utter a variety of purring sounds, one of the commonest being a monotonous and repetitive *cooc-uc-u-coo.*

FOOD

Town pigeons are very adaptable and can survive on spilled food of almost any kind, although grain and other seeds form the bulk of their diet. With this dry food, they need to drink a lot and, in common with other pigeons and doves, they can suck up water without tilting their heads.

NESTING

The birds nest close together in holes and on ledges on all kinds of buildings, often using scraps of paper and plastic and even wire to make simple beds for their eggs. They can bear several broods throughout the year in towns, where temperatures are usually several degrees higher than in the surrounding countryside.

A HELPING HAND

Helping or encouraging town pigeons is not necessary or advisable! They are quite able to look after themselves and many towns discourage the feeding of pigeons because they are already so numerous that their droppings damage buildings. The droppings also create health risks, for the pigeons are known to carry salmonella and several other diseases.

Left: The town pigeon is between 30 and 35cm long.

Above: *In common with all pigeons, the town pigeon flies with rapid wing-beats. Not all individuals have the prominent white rump.*

GREAT SPOTTED WOODPECKER
Dendrocopos major

The large white shoulder flash on each side and the bright red patch under the back end of the body identify this bird. It is a resident in woodlands nearly everywhere, although absent from Ireland and the far north of Scotland. It also inhabits parks, cemeteries, and gardens with mature trees. In common with other woodpeckers, it has a bouncy flight, but it spends most of its time clinging to tree trunks and branches.

Its call is a loud *kick*, often repeated several times at short intervals. The bird also announces its presence and defends its territory with bursts of loud 'drum-rolls', produced by rapidly hammering a trunk or branch with its beak. This drumming, which is heard mainly in the spring, is the woodpecker's idea of a song.

FOOD
Insects and seeds form the bulk of this woodpecker's diet. The insects are mostly dug from tree trunks and branches with the aid of the stout beak and an extremely long tongue. Seeds may be collected on the ground, but conifer seeds are usually obtained by wedging cones into a favourite bark crevice and prising out the seeds. The cones are then removed and dropped at the foot of the tree.

NESTING
Breeding usually begins in April, when male and female excavate a simple chamber in a tree trunk – usually a dead one. The female then lays her eggs in it without bothering to add any nesting material. Excavation may take several days, but the hammering is much less rapid than the territorial drumming.

A HELPING HAND
Great spotted woodpeckers love peanuts and a good way to appreciate their activities is to wedge the nuts into bark crevices or to stuff them into nut logs (see p. 17). You can also tempt them with suet pushed into the logs, and if you add a few dried mealworms the birds will be even happier. The birds will use hole-type nest-boxes if these are at least 30cm deep with a floor diameter of about 15cm. The entrance hole needs to be at least 5cm in diameter, but if the woodpeckers fancy a box with a smaller hole they can easily enlarge the opening!

Below: The great spotted woodpecker is about 25cm long. Only the adult male has the prominent red spot on the back of the head

GREEN WOODPECKER
Picus viridis

The green woodpecker is easily recognized by its red crown and nape and its green back and wings. It is a resident in most parts of Britain apart from northern Scotland, but does not occur in Ireland. Deciduous and mixed woodlands are its principal habitats, as long as these are not too far from open grassland. Town parks and large gardens with mature trees are regularly visited and sometimes harbour nesting birds. Green woodpeckers have a loud laughing or chuckling call – *pew-pew-pew-pew* – which is often uttered in flight and which is responsible for the name 'yaffle' given to the bird in many areas. The birds rarely drum like their great spotted cousins.

FOOD
Although it collects insects and spiders from bark crevices and can also dig insects from deep in the timber, the green wood-pecker feeds mainly on ants and it spends much of its time mopping them up on the ground. Favourite hunting grounds include parks and large lawns.

NESTING
The two sexes collaborate to excavate a burrow in a tree trunk. The burrow is usually over 30cm deep and the female lays her eggs on a bed of wood chips in April or May.

A HELPING HAND
Green woodpeckers will take mealworms from the bird-table and display considerable agility in getting bird-pudding from a tit-bell or a nut-log. Include dried mealworms in your bird pudding to make it even more inviting and nutritious. The birds will use enclosed nest-boxes fixed two metres or more up on tree trunks. The boxes should be about 45cm deep and have a floor diameter of at least 12cm. The entrance hole must be at least 6.5cm across – but such boxes are more likely to be occupied by starlings!

Above: At about 35cm long, this is Britain's largest wood-pecker. This is a male. The female has an entirely black 'moustache' under the eye.

ROOK
Corvus frugilegus

One of the largest birds likely to be seen in the garden, the rook has glossy black plumage, often with a deep blue or purplish sheen, and a conspicuous grey face. It is a resident species, living mainly in lowland areas where there are clumps of tall trees for nesting and large open areas for feeding. Rooks are very sociable birds and are rarely seen singly. Groups are often seen feeding in parks and on playing fields and roadsides. Large flocks congregate to feed on freshly-ploughed land in the winter. The birds are not keen on towns and it is village gardens that are most likely to receive visits. The commonest call is a harsh *caw-caw-caw*.

FOOD

Rooks are omnivorous birds, existing on a variety of fruits and seeds, including cereal grains, as well as insects and earthworms. They also fare quite well on rabbits and other animals killed on the road. They can be a nuisance in orchards,

especially where cherries and plums are grown, but play a more useful role on farmland by eating large numbers of unwelcome cockchafer grubs and leatherjackets.

Above: *The rook is 40-50 cm long. Adults and young are alike, but youngsters have less obvious grey faces. Carrion crows (above left) are similar but have black faces and stouter beaks.*

A HELPING HAND

If there are rookeries in your vicinity, the birds will come to piles of grain in your garden – as long as the pigeons do not get there first! They will also come for raw or cooked meat. There is little else that the gardener can do to help rooks other than refrain from cutting down tall trees. If you have a large garden, you can plant as trees to provide homes for future generations of rooks.

NESTING

Rooks nest in colonies called rookeries and start building or renovating their scruffy-looking tree-top nests as early as February. The nests are made with sticks, interwoven with the topmost twigs and lined with softer materials. They don't look too secure as the branches sway in the wind, but casualties are remarkably rare. A rookery may contain several dozen nests in close proximity.

JACKDAW

Corvus monedula

This small member of the crow family can be distinguished from its relatives by its grey neck and pale eyes as well as by its size. It is a resident of both town and country, seen in woods and parks, farms, and villages, and also on the coast and on roadside verges everywhere. It struts rapidly over the ground in a rather upright manner.

Jackdaws pair for life and are nearly always seen in pairs, although numerous pairs join forces to forage sociably in the fields and also to roost in trees or on buildings in autumn and winter. The birds have no real song but chatter to each other with a variety of calls, including the harsh *chack-chack-chack* that gives the bird its name.

FOOD

Jackdaws eat almost anything, from grain to nestling birds and carrion from road casualties. They steal cherries from orchards and dig into lawns and other grassland for worms and leatherjackets, and on farmland they often follow sheep and snatch up the insects attracted to the animals' droppings.

NESTING

The jackdaw's natural nesting sites are holes in trees or rocks, but the birds are more than happy to occupy holes in buildings and they not uncommonly cause problems by nesting in chimneys. Being fairly sociable birds, they often build close together. The nest itself is an untidy cluster of twigs lined with grass and wool or hair. Eggs are laid from May onwards.

A HELPING HAND

Although the jackdaws' aerobatic antics are fascinating to watch, their attacks on fruit and smaller birds make them unpopular with some people and not everyone wants to attract them to the garden – but they will come anyway if you put out food for other birds. Meat and cheese are particularly attractive to them. Providing open-fronted nest-boxes on trees or walls may prevent them from nesting in your chimney. The boxes should have a floor at least 20cm square. The birds will also use closed boxes as long as the entrance hole is at least 15cm across.

Below: The jackdaw is 30-35cm long, with adults and juveniles all having similar plumage. The short, but sturdy beak is able to deal with all kinds of food.

MAGPIE
Pica pica

With its long tail and bold black and white plumage, the magpie is an unmistakable bird that has become more numerous in recent years. It is resident in many habitats, including towns and villages, but is perhaps most common in areas with scattered trees or tall hedges and plenty of open grassland.

Few town parks are without their resident magpies, which are usually seen in small groups. Their most common call is a rather harsh *chack*, which is often repeated rapidly to produce a rattle-like chatter. The soft warbling song is rarely heard.

FOOD
Magpies are scavengers, eating almost anything they can find. They are often seen feasting on carrion on the road, and they regularly take eggs and nestlings from other birds' nests. This last habit has led to accusations that magpies have

Below: The magpie is 40-50cm long, including its tail. Although it appears black and white from a distance, the dark feathers have beautiful blue and green iridescence on closer view.

been responsible for the recent decline in many of our garden birds, but there is no proof that magpies have had more than a minimal effect. The birds also eat large numbers of insects, and take fruit in the autumn.

NESTING
Magpies nest mainly in trees and tall hedges, building an untidy cup with twigs and mud and then roofing it with a dome of twigs. The cup is lined with fine roots and hair and eggs are laid from April onwards.

Nests may be built in holes or in dense creepers on houses.

A HELPING HAND
Few people will want to encourage magpies into the garden because of their predatory habits, but they will come anyway if there is a chance of food. Avoid putting out large chunks of food, especially meat: chop it into small pieces and the magpies will show less interest.

JAY

Garrulus glandarius

This colourful member of the crow family is easily recognized by its pinkish brown back, the chequered blue front edge of the wing and the white rump. It is resident nearly everywhere apart from northern Scotland. Essentially a woodland bird, it is rarely seen far from trees and is likely to visit only well-timbered gardens. It can also be seen in town parks and churchyards with mature trees, but you are likely to hear the harsh warning call – *shark-shark-shark* – usually uttered in flight, before you see the bird itself. Jays are also good mimics of other birds and even human voices.

FOOD

The jay is an omnivorous bird with a general preference for fruits and seeds and it can be a nuisance in orchards. Acorns are among its favourite foods and it can hold up to nine at a time – one in its beak and the rest in a pouch in its throat. It buries lots of acorns in the autumn – as many as 150 in a day – to serve as a larder for the winter, but not all of them are recovered so the jay can be held responsible for at least some regeneration of our oak woods! Jays also eat plenty of insects and other small animals, including mice and voles, and occasionally take eggs and nestlings from other birds' nests.

in the forks of trees, often quite low down, and consist mainly of twigs and mud with a lining of roots and hair. Eggs are laid from April onwards and the youngsters are fed mainly with caterpillars.

Below: The jay is about 35cm long. The sexes are alike, but juvenile birds lack the streaked head feathers. The white rump patch and the white wing-bars are very conspicuous when the birds are in flight.

NESTING

Jays nest mainly in woodland, but occasionally use parks and orchards, and even tall hedgerows. Twenty or more birds may gather at the start of the breeding season for a bit of communal courting, during which they all warble softly to each other before pairing up and nesting. The nests are built

A HELPING HAND

Jays may visit your garden if this does not involve straying too far from the trees, and you can encourage them by putting fruit and nuts on the lawn or on a ground-station. Scatter some acorns around and watch the birds cram them into their throat pouches. Jays also enjoy mealworms, but don't expect them to nest in any but the largest and most mature of gardens.

HOUSE MARTIN

Delichon urbica

The house martin has glossy blue-black upper parts, a white rump and an almost pure white underside, but it is difficult to appreciate this when you see the bird streaking through the air 100 metres or more above the ground. You have to rely on its short forked tail to distinguish it from the superficially similar swallow. It is a summer visitor, usually arriving from Africa towards the end of April and nesting in towns and villages all over the country. It can also be found in upland and coastal areas where there are suitable cliffs for nesting. Populations have fallen in recent years – possibly the result of prolonged droughts and a shortage of insects in parts of Africa – but house martins can still be seen over most gardens in the summer. They utter a variety of twittering calls both in flight and at their nests, and a large colony can be quite noisy. The birds fly back to Africa in September and October.

FOOD

House martins are entirely insectivorous and spend nearly all of their time on the wing scooping flies and other small insects from the air with their wide-open beaks.

NESTING

The original nesting sites of house martins were cliffs, but most of the birds now nest on buildings, often in large colonies. The cup-shaped nests are made with mud, reinforced with roots and other plant fibres and lined with feathers. They are fixed under the eaves or other overhangs, with just a small opening at the top. Two or three broods are reared from late May onwards. The birds return to the same nest sites year after year.

A HELPING HAND

House martins are obviously not interested in anything on the bird-table, but you can encourage them to nest on your house by fixing special 'martin boxes' under the eaves.

Above: House martins are about 14cm long; the sexes are alike. Juveniles lack the bluish sheen.

You can make your own boxes (see page 21), or you can buy ready-made plastic ones. These boxes also attract house sparrows, so if you want to reserve space for the martins it is a good idea to block up the entrances until the martins arrive. Artificial homes are most likely to be used in areas lacking a supply of natural mud. You can also help by providing some mud in an old dustbin lid or simply by soaking an area of your garden every day during the building season.

SWALLOW

Hirundo rustica

The swallow is closely related to the house martin, from which it can be distinguished by its red face and throat and very long forked tail. It is a summer visitor, usually arriving from Africa in April and leaving again around the beginning of September. Favouring open country, it is most likely to be seen around farms and villages, especially adjacent to ponds and streams.

As with the house martin, a recent fall in the population has been blamed on drought in parts of Africa. Swallows give out a sharp *vit-vit-vit* in flight and also have a squeaky, twittering song. The latter is uttered in long sequences and can be quite loud when large numbers gather on the telephone wires prior to migration. The birds also roost communally in reed beds at this time.

FOOD

Swallows are entirely insectivorous, catching mosquitoes and other small insects in mid-air just like house martins do, although they often operate at lower levels than the martins.

NESTING

Originally nesting in caves, swallows now make use of bridges and other buildings, especially barns, church towers and porches, and also railway stations. They like to be under cover and they also need some degree of support under their nests. Girders and rafters are popular nesting sites. The nest is a shallow cup of mud and dried grass, lined with feathers. Town houses provide few suitable sites, so swallows are less common in towns than house martins. Two or three broods are reared from May onwards.

A HELPING HAND

You are unlikely to be able to lure swallows with food, but you can encourage them to nest inside a shed or barn by fixing a shallow wooden box or

Above and left: *The swallow is about 19cm long, including its tail, and has a bluer back than the house martin. The sexes are alike. Juveniles have shorter tails and pale pink faces.*

even half a coconut shell to a shelf or rafter – as long as there is clear access to it. Provide mud in an old dustbin lid or soak an area of the garden regularly to provide natural building materials.

PIED WAGTAIL
Motacilla alba

The pied wagtail can be recognized by its white face and black crown and by its long and constantly wagging tail. It is a common resident of towns and villages and also lives in open country, especially near water. Few parks and large lawns are without one or two of these lively little birds darting hither and thither. They spend most of their time on the ground, although large numbers may gather to roost in urban trees on winter nights. The main call, uttered in flight, is a high-pitched *chizzick*, while the song is a prolonged warble during which the call sound is modified in various ways.

Left: The pied wagtail is about 18cm long. Females, juveniles, and winter males are greyer than the summer male pictured here. All have white throats in the winter. Pied wagtails are very nimble birds, and walk with a jerky gait while the tail never stops wagging.

A HELPING HAND
Pied wagtails frequently scavenge crumbs and small seeds under the bird-table in the winter and will appreciate crushed biscuits and cereal products on a ground-station. Some birds may become tame enough to feed from your hand. They also appreciate your pond, for bathing and for the abundant insects flying around it at all times of the year. They will occupy open-fronted nest-boxes with a floor area of about 12cm square, and you can also encourage them by removing a brick or a stone from an old wall to leave a cavity, as long as it is fairly well concealed.

FOOD
Pied wagtails feed almost entirely on insects, which they snap up on or close to the ground or sometimes over water. Open grassland is the favourite hunting ground, but the birds can also be seen foraging on roads and pavements, where they find small seeds and scraps dropped by people. These foods undoubtedly augment the insect supply in the winter and make it easier for the birds to survive. Large numbers of pied wagtails die in hard winters when the ground is covered with snow.

NESTING
The cup-shaped nest is built in some sort of cavity, often in an old wall or a river bank, and it is made largely of twigs, leaves, and moss with a lining of hair or feathers. One or two broods are reared from May onwards.

SPOTTED FLYCATCHER
Muscicapa striata

This slender greyish brown bird is sometimes mistaken for a female house sparrow, although it has a much more slender beak and a paler underside. The breast is clearly streaked and there is no white wing-bar. It is one of the latest of our summer visitors, arriving from southern Africa in late May or June and usually leaving again at the beginning of September. It settles in woods and parks and many gardens – wherever there are trees and shrubs with plenty of open spaces between them. The main call is a somewhat scratchy *tsee-tsee-tsee*, often followed by one or two clicks, and the song is a fairly quiet medley of call-like sounds.

FOOD
As its name suggests, the spotted flycatcher feeds on insects. Hover-flies make up a large proportion of its diet, but it does not confine itself to flies and will eat almost any insect that it can catch, including bees and wasps and even butterflies. The bird watches from a prominent perch and darts out to snap up anything that comes within range. It may hover for a second or two before returning to its perch to enjoy its meal. In cool weather, when few insects are on the wing, the flycatcher will search for insects on the foliage of trees and shrubs.

NESTING
The bird normally breeds on concealed ledges – often among creepers on a wall – where it builds a cup-shaped nest with grass and other plant material and lines it with hair or feathers. Eggs are laid in May or June and a second brood may be raised later in the summer.

A HELPING HAND
Spotted flycatchers obviously take no interest in bird-table food, but you can certainly encourage them with open-fronted nest-boxes having a floor area of 10cm square. The birds will also use simple tunnels of the type described for house sparrows (p. 26).

Below: The spotted flycatcher is about 15cm long with quite short legs and a relatively large head. Adults and juveniles all look more or less alike, although juveniles are more spotty on the back. The flycatcher is not at all worried by the stings of bees and wasps: it merely pulls them out before eating the insects.

TAWNY OWL
Strix aluco

This rusty brown or greyish brown owl (length c.40cm) resides in wooded areas, including parks and churchyards, all over Britain, but not in Ireland. At rest in trees in the daytime, it is beautifully camouflaged against the bark. The shrill *kee-wick* is its best-known call, and there is also a hooting 'song' – *too-woo-woo-woo*. The legendary *tuwit-too-woo* is likely to be produced by two birds, one calling *kee-wick* and the other replying in song.

FOOD
Voles and beetles are the owl's main prey, located with amazing eyesight and acute hearing and snatched from the ground after a silent swoop. House sparrows are often caught in urban areas.

NESTING
Tawny owls breed in March or April, usually in tree holes or crevices where they lay their eggs without making a nest. If you have large trees in your garden tawny owls may settle in deep nest-boxes fixed to the trunks or slung under the branches.

LITTLE OWL
Athene noctua

Because of its largely diurnal habits and its liking for perching on exposed poles and fences, this owl is more likely to be seen than its larger cousins. It can be recognized by its small size (length c.25cm) and its white 'eye-brows'. Introduced to Britain in the 19th century, it now resides in open country all over southern Britain and often hunts over parks, hedgerows, and large gardens. Its main call is a shrill *keeooo-keeooo-keeooo*, with a drop in pitch and volume towards the end of each phrase.

FOOD
The little owl eats a wide range of small animals, especially insects and small birds.

NESTING
The little owl's nest is an unlined hole, usually in a tree but sometimes in a wall or among rocks, or even in the ground. The bird may even take over an old nest of another bird. Eggs are laid from April onwards.

BARN OWL
Tyto alba

The light brown back and pure white underside, combined with the heart-shaped white face, readily identify this handsome owl (length c.35-40cm). It lives on farmland and in other open habitats nearly all over the country, although it is absent from much of the Highlands. The bird is also known as the screech owl, because of its harsh screeching calls. After a drastic decline in numbers during the second half of the 20th century, the population is now increasing – partly due to the provision of nest-boxes.

FOOD
The barn owl feeds mainly on mice and other small mammals, but also catches house sparrows around farms and other buildings at dusk. In common with other owls, it has soft-edged feathers that cut silently through the air, so the prey has no warning of the owl's approach.

NESTING
Barn owls make no nests. They simply lay their eggs in holes in trees, rocks, or old buildings, including barns, although the eggs may be cushioned on a pile of soft pellets coughed up by the adults. The birds can be encouraged to nest in a barn by fixing an old tea chest to the ceiling.

WAXWING
Bombycilla garrulus

Named for the waxy red blobs on its wings, this uncommon winter visitor (length c.20cm) can also be recognized by the crest on its head and the pale yellow band at the tip of its tail. The birds breed in the coniferous forests of the far north and move south for the winter. They are most likely to be seen in northern and eastern parts of British Isles, but they may not appear at all in mild winters. The birds produce a fairly musical call, and a flock can be quite noisy if the birds all call at once.

FOOD
Waxwings feed mainly on fruits and seeds. They occasionally visit bird tables offering dried fruits, but are more likely to be seen scouring the hedgerows and shrubberies for tasty berries. They are particularly fond of rowan and firethorn fruits. Town parks and well-planted car parks sometimes attract small flocks.

SISKIN
Carduelis spinus

The siskin is a small (length c.12cm), mainly black and yellow finch. Its yellow rump is clearly seen in flight, and there is also a clear yellow stripe across its dark wings. The back and sides are streaked. It breeds mainly in the coniferous forests of the north and west, but in the winter it spreads all over the country and this is when it is most likely to be seen in the garden, although it is not common. Siskins are fairly noisy birds, chattering with a variety of calls which in winter include quite a 'scratchy' *tsoo-tsoo* that sometimes falls and sometimes rises at the end.

FOOD

Conifer seeds and insects are the siskin's main foods, with the small seeds of birch and alder seeds very important in the winter. Siskins appreciate peanuts and other seeds in the garden and are very clever at extracting them from a range of feeders.

NESTING

The nest, usually built high in coniferous trees, is a cup of twigs and vegetation lined with hair and feathers. There are usually two broods, each with up to six nestlings.

REDSTART
Phoenicurus phoenicurus

The redstart (length c.14cm) is named for the bright rust-red tail feathers, best seen when the bird is in flight but also visible when the bird flicks its tail while perched. It arrives from Africa in April and spends the summer with us before returning to Africa in September. It likes wooded habitats, including parks and churchyards and large gardens. The redstart's main call is a whistling *whooit-whooit-tuk-tuk-tuk*.

FOOD

Redstarts feed mainly on insects and spiders. Hen birds find most of their food on the ground or on vegetation but males show off their agility by snatching insects in mid-air. The birds also eat soft berries.

NESTING

Redstarts breed in holes in trees and walls, often at ground level. Their rather untidy nests are built with grass and other vegetation and lined with feathers. The hen usually lays her eggs towards the end of May and may produce another clutch later in the summer.

FIELDFARE

Turdus pilaris

In most parts of the British Isles the fieldfare is a winter visitor, arriving from the north in late autumn and staying until the spring. It resembles a song thrush (length c.25cm) but has a grey head and a grey rump. Fieldfares are very social birds, often forming flocks of a dozen or more as they search gardens and hedgerows for haws and other fruits and chuckle to each other with bursts of *chack-chack-chack-chack*. The birds tend to be most numerous in gardens in the coldest winters.

FOOD
Fieldfares eat lots of worms and insects in the summer, but their winter diet consists mainly of fruit taken from hedgerows and shrubberies. You can encourage them into your garden by leaving fallen apples on the grass. Dried fruit and bird-pudding will attract fieldfares to your bird-table in snowy weather, when fruits are hard to find.

NESTING
Fieldfares have started to breed in the north of Britain in recent years, but this is still a rare event. The nest is a bulky cup, made largely from grass and mud. It is built on the ground or in a tree and there may be several nests in close proximity.

REDWING

Turdus iliacus

The redwing (length c.20cm) gets its name for the red patch on each flank and under each wing. Apart from that, it looks like a song thrush, although it has a more obvious pale stripe above each eye. Redwings are winter visitors from northern Europe and are most likely to be seen searching for fruit in the hedgerows – often in large flocks. They generally visit our gardens only in really cold or snowy weather. The commonest call at this time is a musical *swip-swip swip*, but there is also a high-pitched *see-see-see* that is usually produced in flight.

FOOD
Redwings feed on a wide range of hedgerow fruits in autumn and winter. They also eat lots of insects, worms, and other small ground-living creatures. A good way to encourage them into your garden is to scatter apples on the lawn. The birds may also take dried fruit and mealworms from the bird-table.

NESTING
Although redwings have occasionally nested in Scotland, the birds usually breed in the forests of northern Europe. The nest is a cup of grass and moss, often built on the ground.

BLACKCAP
Sylvia atricapilla

The blackcap is named for the male's jet-black cap. The rest of his body (length c.15cm) displays various shades of grey. Females have rusty brown caps. Until fairly recently, blackcaps were purely summer visitors to the British Isles, but more now stay with us through the winter, mainly in Wales and the south-west. During the summer they occur in most areas, frequenting woods, parks, and gardens with plenty of shrubs and undergrowth. They have a rich, flute-like song as well as a harsh *tek-tek-tek* call that sounds like two pebbles being knocked together.

FOOD
Insects and spiders are the blackcap's main foods in spring and summer, but berries take over later in the year. The birds are especially fond of elderberries. Food is generally gathered directly from the vegetation. Blackcaps are not very interested in bird-tables. They may visit them in winter for dried fruit, suet, and mealworms, but the best way to attract these birds is to grow various berry-bearing shrubs.

NESTING
The nest is a neat cup, made from dry grass, moss, and hair and fixed in a dense bush or hedge. There is usually just one brood. The birds show little interest in nest-boxes, although they do sometimes build on ledges in disused outbuildings.

MARSH TIT
Parus palustris

At first sight, the marsh tit (length c.12cm) might be mistaken for a blackcap, but it can be distinguished by its white neck and black 'bib'. It is a woodland bird, despite its name, and is a common resident in mature woodlands, parks, and large gardens in England and Wales. It is absent from Ireland and from most of Scotland. Its best-known call is a bell-like *pi-choo*, the second syllable of which may be quite long.

FOOD
Marsh tits eat a variety of soft fruits, seeds, and insects. They visit bird-tables and other feeders in the winter and are particularly fond of peanuts and sunflower seeds. They are most likely to be seen in gardens close to woodlands or those with plenty of trees. A good way to encourage the birds into your garden is to plant various berry-bearing shrubs, such as bird cherry and mirabelle plum.

NESTING
Marsh tits normally nest in holes in trees, where they build mossy cups lined with hair and feathers. The birds will happily move into enclosed nest-boxes with entrance holes about 28mm in diameter. The female lays her eggs in May and sometimes rears a second brood later in the summer.

SPARROWHAWK

Accipiter nisus

The grey wings and barred rather than spotted breast distinguish this bird from the kestrel. In flight, it can be distinguished by its shorter and broader wings. The bird (length 30-40cm) is most likely to be seen swooping rapidly and silently along the hedgerow or through the shrubbery in search of small birds. It is a resident species but its call – *kew-kew-kew* – is rarely heard outside the breeding season.

FOOD

True to its name, the sparrowhawk feeds mainly on sparrows and other small birds, which it catches in mid-air or snatches from the bird-table. This makes it unwelcome in many gardens, but there is nothing you can do to keep it out and it can be argued that the sparrowhawk actually does some good by weeding out the weaklings. Some people are therefore happy to see this handsome and agile hunter around the garden.

NESTING

They lay their eggs on a loose platform of twigs wedged into a tree. If you have a garden with mature trees you can encourage a pair to settle down by placing a wooden platform in one of the trees.

KESTREL

Falco tinnunculus

With its long tail and pointed wings, this resident hunter (length c.25cm) is one of our commonest birds of prey. It is most likely to be seen hovering over open fields and roadside verges as it searches for its prey. It is also quite happy in town parks, and it will certainly come to the garden if there is a chance of food – but its main targets here are the smaller birds on your bird-table, so it is not always a welcome visitor. A shrill *kee-kee-kee* is the commonest call, but the kestrel keeps quiet for most of the time. It is best distinguished from the sparrowhawk by its brown wings and speckled rather than barred breast.

FOOD

Voles are the kestrel's main prey. Incredibly sharp eyes allow the bird to spot the animals while hovering as much as 15 metres up in the air, or perhaps when perched on trees or telephone wires, and it then plunges down to snatch them from the ground. Birds and insects, especially beetles, are eaten less often, although sparrows and starings make up most of the kestrel's food in urban habitats.

NESTING

Kestrels breed in April or May, either in holes or on ledges, on cliffs and buildings as well as in trees. The eggs are laid on a flimsy mat of grass or leaves if they are lucky. If you have tall buildings or mature trees in your garden you might be able to tempt a kestrel to move into a large open-fronted nest-box. This needs to have a floor area of about 45cm square and it should be fixed at least 5 metres above the ground.

INDEX

PICTURE CREDITS

The publisher wishes to express sincere thanks to **John Daniels** of Shoot! Photographic, who took many of the published pictures specifically for this book. Thanks are also due to **Gardman Ltd** who kindly provided a selection of their bird feeders for photography.

Michael Chinery: 7 top right.
John Daniels: 1 bottom, 2 bottom left, 3, 7 top inset, 9 top right, 11 bottom, 12 bottom left, 13 food sequence, 14 bottom left, 14 top right, 15 feeders, 15 top inset, 16 all, 17 all, 18 bottom, 19 centre, 19 bottom right, 20, 21 top, 21 bottom right, 22 right, 24 centre right, 25 top left, 26 centre right, 27 top inset, 28 centre right, 29 centre right, 30 top inset left, 30 centre right, 31 top inset right, 32 centre left, 32 centre right, 33 top inset right, 34 top inset right, 34 bottom, 35 top inset right, 36 bottom, 37 top inset left, 37 centre right, 38 top inset right, 39 centre right, 39 bottom, 40 top inset, 40 bottom centre, 41 centre right, 41 bottom centre, 43 centre right, 44 centre right, 45 bottom right, 46 bottom, 47 top inset, 47 centre, 48 top inset, 48 centre left, 49 bottom, 50 bottom, 51 top inset, 51 centre, 52 top inset, 52 centre right, 52 bottom left, 53 top inset, 53 centre right, 53 bottom, 54 top inset, 54 centre left, 55 top inset, 55 bottom right, 56 top inset, 56 centre right, 56 bottom, 57 top inset, 57 centre left, 58 top inset, 58 bottom left, 59 top inset, 59 centre right, 59 bottom left, 60 top inset, 60 bottom left, 61 top inset right.
Interpet Publishing: 22 centre left.
iStockPhoto.com
   AtWaG: 2 top inset.
   Charlie Bishop: 24 bottom.
   Aleksander Bolbot: 30 centre left.
   Sue Colvil: 19 top inset.
   Jacques Croizer: 9 top inset.
   Chris Downie: 21 top inset.
   Janet Forjan-Freedman: 8 top left.
   Hannah Gleg: 41 inset feather.

   Gertan Hooijer: 18 top, 49 top inset left, 57 bottom.
   Pamela Hodson: 29 top inset left.
   Andrew Howe: 1 top, 2 top right, 15 bottom right, 26 top inset both, 27 bottom, 28 top inset left, 28 bottom right, 29 top inset right, 31 top inset left, 31 centre left, 32 top inset both, 33 top inset left, 33 bottom left, 34 top inset left, 35 top inset left, 35 centre, 36 top inset, 37 top inset right, 37 bottom, 38 top inset left, 38 centre right, 38 bottom right, 39 top inset, 40 centre left, 41 top inset, 42 both, 43 top inset, 44 top inset, 44 bottom left, 46 top inset, 50 top inset, 58 centre right, 61 top inset left.
   Iwka: 8 centre.
   Alastair Johnson: 7 top left.
   Jim Jurica: 25 top inset.
   Kalulu: 45 top inset.
   Cay-Uwe Kulzer: 10 bottom left.
   Lubilub: 9 top left.
   Themi Mintzas: 23 top left.
   Thomas Mounsey: 55 inset wasp.
   Nsjulio: 23 top inset.
   Michael Owen: 56 inset mouse.
   Mark Penny: 61 bottom right.
   Stephanie Phillips: 11 top inset.
   Hazel Proudlove: 9 centre.
   Stephen Rees: 11 top centre, 30 top inset right.
   Terry Robilliard: 10 top right.
   Willi Schmitz: 12 top right, 34 centre.
   David Shawley: 48 centre right.
   Olga Shelego: 19 inset feather, 27 inset feather.
   Nigel Silcock: 8 bottom right.
   Michal Szota: 45 centre.
   Nancy Tunison: 23 centre right.
   Roger Whiteway: 24 top left.
   WinterWitch: 49 top inset right.
   Tammy Wolfe: 13 top inset.

Shutterstock
   Darren Baker: 6-7.